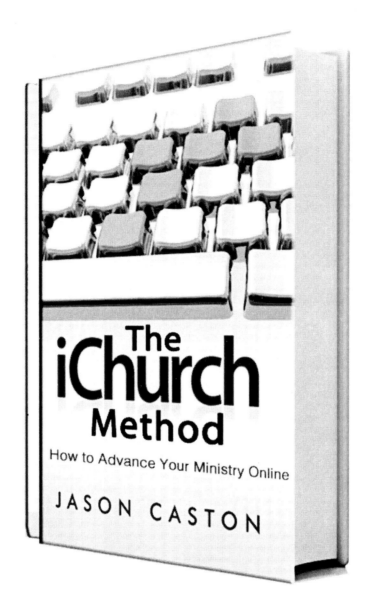

The iChurch Method
How to Advance Your Ministry Online

www.TheiChurchMethod.com

www.facebook.com/ichurchmethod

www.twitter.com/ichurchmethod

2012 Edition – v2

Caston Digital Books

Copyright © 2012 by Caston Digital LLC

ISBN-10: 0615589642

ISBN-13: 978-0615589640

Written By: Jason Caston

Cover Design: www.sohocreative.com

Dedication

This book is dedicated to the ministries that gave me the opportunity to showcase my gifts: Crenshaw Christian Center, The Potter's House of Dallas, Fellowship Church and Saddleback Church. The people that supported me most from the concept of this book to the actual manifestation: my wife Demetra Caston, my mom Sylvia Coleman, my buddy Pastor Paula Smith, my mentor Minister Henry Abraham and all my friends and family. The Father, who gave me a purpose that was greater than I thought I would ever be, My Savior who came so that I could have life and have it more abundantly, and My Helper who gives me revelation that surpasses all understanding and the power to accomplish more than I could have ever imagined.

The iChurch Method Online Network

You can also join The iChurch Method Online Network at http://www.theichurchmethod.com/network/ which is an online training membership network that offers online training courses, training videos, newsletters, webinars, early access to new books, products and services and exclusive access to sessions with author Jason Caston.

Technology Disclaimer

Since the focus of this book is not just strategy but also technology, there is the possibility that some websites and technologies may change within this book. I decided to include actual technologies, specific websites and online software because I wanted to walk ministries through actually how to use them and not just speak in general strategy terms and hope churches figured it out. With that approach comes the benefit of a dual approach of strategy and technology but the drawback of a website updating and some of my images and steps being outdated. Thus, I will update this book as often as possible to stay current with technologies and keep the latest version in print as well as available via the iChurch Method website and the iChurch Method Online Network. Thanks and I hope this book is a blessing to you, your church and/or ministry.

Table of Contents

Part 3 Ecommerce – Online Stores/Online Donations

Part 4 Social Media – Engage and Connect

Part 5 Mobile – The Future of Technology and Ministry

Introduction

The purpose of this book is simple: to help ministries advance the Kingdom online and take the gospel to the world. This is quite a goal. But, thank God for technology because understanding and using it properly will help us all achieve this goal.

Whether you are a storefront church or an individual with a ministry, you can have an online presence that is similar to the largest megachurch. Believe it! The online tools that are available today have empowered the individual with solutions. The solutions usually have minimal or no costs. No longer are we restricted by finances and large development teams in order to create a great web presence. Can I get an Amen? With this book, a storefront can have an internet church that is as good as or better than the largest mega-church on earth.

So how do I get **The iChurch Method** from my brain to yours? That's a good question. I started thinking about it and realized that I would have two separate and distinct audiences. The first reader I considered was the *decision maker*. This reader may be in church management (deacon, elder, vestry) and part of a larger group. Or the reader may run a ministry and be the sole decision maker. Either way, the decision maker needs to know what options are available, the benefits, the costs, how long it will take and other such details to make an informed decision when setting the strategy. For the decision makers, I have written as plainly as I could using easy-to-understand examples for clear communication. In each Part, the first section is totally devoted to the decision maker. Technical matters are non-existent. My "big idea" is that the decision maker will read the first section of each Part and much like a cafeteria, select which pieces of the iChurch fit their strategy. Each of these sections is called *Let's Talk Strategy*. At the end of the Let's Talk Strategy section, I have recapped the strategy choices by listing them all out. This list is called: *What I Want For My iChurch*. My hope is that you, the decision maker, will copy that page and highlight the items you want for your iChurch and then hand it off for implementation to the *technical person* who happens to be my second audience. For the techie, I have written the second part of each Part called *Let's Talk*

Tech. This is written with programming language and code that an average technical person can handle. No doubt there are some decision makers who will have the skill necessary to accomplish some of the technical items. For those folks, they have the good fortune of being able to read and understand the entire book. So, before you start reading, classify yourself and head to the appropriate section.

During or after you have read this book, your feedback, comments and questions would be appreciated. You can email me at **caston@ichurchmethod.com**. Depending on the volume, I will do my best to get back with you. Of course, you can always hire Caston Digital via the services tab at http://www.theichurchmethod.com to complete all or parts of your iChurch. You can also join The iChurch Method Online Network at http://www.theichurchmethod.com/network/ which is an online training membership network that offers online training courses, training videos, newsletters, webinars, early access to new books, products and services and exclusive access to sessions with author Jason Caston.

Now on to the journey.......*"I must proclaim the **good news** of the kingdom of God to the other towns also, because that is why I was sent."* Luke 4:43

So now the question is, what is the "iChurch Method?" It's a five part approach to taking your ministry online and reaching the world:

Part 1: Website – A Great Website that is Easy-to-Use.

Part 2: Multimedia – Interactive Multimedia.

Part 3: Ecommerce – Online Stores/Online Donations.

Part 4: Social Media – Engage and Connect.

Part 5: Mobile – The Future of Technology and Ministry.

With these five parts, a ministry can reach and change the world. That is the power of The iChurch Method. Let's get started.

Part 1
A Great Website that is Easy-To-Use

Let's Talk Strategy

Why Is A Website Important?

In today's world of smartphones, iPads and laptops, let's agree on one thing: before a visitor sets foot in your church, the odds are incredibly high that she will first look at your website. There are many reasons why this happens. This visitor may be needing directions. They may be looking at the membership size. They may not be able to attend in person and want to view your services online. But more than likely, the visitor wants a glimpse of what's inside; what to expect when they arrive at your front door.

The "fear of the unknown" can be a powerful deterrent to potential visitors. With an engaging, professional, innovative website, the visitor will feel comfortable getting into their car, driving to your church and walking inside. If the visitor wants to view your service online, your iChurch website will make it easy for them. A quality website will accomplish <u>all</u> of these goals. It will put aside those fears and breakdown any barriers allowing the visitor to have an opportunity to become a member of God's Kingdom. And expanding the Kingdom is what it's all about. Right?

Hopefully, you fully understand why a website is so very important. Most likely, you already have a website. If so, great! You are ahead of the game. If you still lack a website, worry no more because this book has you covered.

What are the Objectives for a Church Website?

A church's website has three main *objectives*: (a) help people find a church to attend (online or in-person); (b) inform potential and active church members of the current ministries and events; and (c) provide spiritual content that helps people grow in their faith. These objectives would be different if the website was selling shoes. A shoe store would have objectives like: (a) help shoppers find the right shoe; (b) convince the shopper to come into the store to buy the shoes or purchase them online; and (c) provide tips on good shoe care. If you are running a Christian Missions ministry, your website objectives might be: (a) inform visitors about the need for ministry work in Haiti; (b) explain what the ministry is currently doing in Haiti; (c) request donations through an online payment system. For every category of website, there is a different set of objectives.

If you do not have a website, please use the above objectives as a guide for your site. If you have a website, see how it stacks up against the above objectives. Whether or not you have a website, it is critical that you list out your church or ministry's objectives and see if your site meets them. Please understand that not all churches and ministries will have the same objectives. Don't worry if your objectives don't line up exactly with the ones above.

Once you establish the objectives for the website, we need to move to *design criteria*. The good news is that all websites have one thing in common: they should all have the same design criteria. The design criteria should be: (a) clean or uncluttered (not busy); (b) informative by providing helpful content; (c) cause the user to interact with the website; (d) engaging and interesting; and (e) provide solutions via products, content and/or multimedia.

This *design criteria* is a lot to get your mind around. To give you a clearer understanding of these, let's look at a website that is a good example of all the above-mentioned objectives and design criteria.

The Potter's House Church of Dallas: A Great Ministry Website Example
The Potter's House of Dallas, Inc. has an excellent website for us to look at, http://www.thepottershouse.org. TPHD is a church website I know well because I help develop and maintain it. Bishop T.D. Jakes and his web staff understand the importance of an engaging website and to no surprise, this website hits all the targets.

THE POTTER'S HOUSE

| Home | Local | National | Multi-Media | News | Store | Donate | Locations | ▶ |

SundayWorship

The Potter's House is a multi-cultural, dynamic, and engaging non-denominational church.

1 2 3 4 5 6

MEGA CARE   TEXT MESSAGE UPDATES   Potter's House LIVE WATCH NOW   OTHER LOCATIONS

WELCOME TO THE POTTER'S HOUSE

Our prayer for you is that the God of all grace anoints you with fresh oil and His precious Spirit illuminates the Word as you read. May He empower you to effectively communicate to others the vibrant hope that He has given you to persevere the struggles that you have overcome and continue to overcome.

Furthermore, my wife and I pray that your home be a reflection of the joy and peace that God has promised to all of His children who follow Him. We bless your children, the fruit of your body. We speak life into your marriage, your ministry and your mission.

As you lie down at night we pray for more than sleep. We pray for rest. Rest in Him and arise refreshed for we need you. Your prayers, your support and your love are important to us. So we pray you will take care of yourself.

-Bishop and Mrs. T. D. Jakes

DONATIONS
Send a secure online gift today.

I AM NEW
Learn more. ▶

SHARE TPH
Learn more. ▶

Worship Times	**Self Help Section**	**Contact Infomation**

Sunday- 9:00 a.m. CST
Wednesday - 7:00 p.m. CST

Life is tough. Sometimes in spite of our best efforts we are still overwhelmed. At such times we need someone to reflect our Savior in the trenches of our inner battles and interpersonal struggles. The mission of The Potter's House Counseling Center is to walk with you every step of the way as you seek spiritual and emotional wholeness. Programs & Information include:

| Counseling Services | Special Programs | Special Messages |
| Post Traumatic Stress | HIV/AIDS Awareness Efforts | Spiritual Enrichment Groups |

Phone:
1.800.BISHOP2

Address:
6777 W. Kiest Blvd.
Dallas, TX 75236-3006
Map This

E-mail:
custservice@tdjakes.org

Home

Local
Visitors
About Us
Local Ministries
Events and Calendar
Community
TPH Insiders
Contact Us

National
Conferences
MegaCare
Partners
PHIPA
The Potter's Touch
Events & Meetings
TPH Insiders
TDJ Insiders

Multimedia
How to Watch
Live Streaming - Computer
Live Service Iphone-Ipad
The Potter's House News
Television Broadcast
The Potter's Touch
Internet Church
Radio
Share TPH Online

Press
Awards & Honors
TPH Press Kit
Press Release Archive
Forms

VeriSign Secured
VERIFY+
Privacy | Terms & Conditions

Let's look at the design criteria first and see how it stacks up against ThePottersHouse.org

Clean and Uncluttered - For a website that has many areas you can explore, this is quite clean. The more options and content a site has, the higher the clutter factor but this website seems to have a good mix of content and imagery. The top menu is clean with buttons that are easy to read. The large banners in the middle are great visual eye-catchers and hold users attention. The four sub buttons that are beneath the banners showcase what the ministry is doing and how to connect, online or offline. When you consider how many options the site provides, I feel this website strikes the right design balance between cleanliness and volume of options and content.

Informative by Providing Helpful Content - Another direct hit. Beneath the four sub buttons that are beneath the large banners there are three vertically stacked tabs on the right. These show very important topics, especially the "donations" and the "I am New". These three vertical tabs provide a new visitor with a great starting point to connect with the ministry. Lastly, the bottom boxes showcase service times, self help section and service times, these buttons are consistent on all pages and provide important information for this ministry. Look at the incredible choices. Everything I can think of is covered there. This site is highly informative and helpful!

Cause the User to Interact With the Website - Let's be honest here, don't you feel like clicking on one of the large banners, four sub buttons or three vertical tabs? Or at least scrolling down to the self-help section and finding a link to check out? I do. Once a visitor starts interacting with your website, chances are excellent that they we will visit your church in person.

Engaging and Interesting – The large banner of "Sunday Worship" is certainly engaging. The overall color scheme is pleasing to the eye. Also, there are essentially two colors besides the standard black and white: purple and blue, although it's not noticeable since we published this book in black and white but take our word for it: that's it. As for *interesting*, the content choices meet that criteria. The bottom line is this site is very engaging and interesting.

Provide Solutions via Products, Content or Multimedia - The Potter's House of Dallas website meets this requirement by having the following buttons:

- I Am New button – this button leads to *content* that is geared towards educating new people on the church.
- Watch Now button – this button leads to *multimedia* that the user can watch and interact with.
- Self Help Section – this section focuses on the topics that many people deal with and provide *content* to help them resolve these issues.
- Multi-Media menu option at the top - this button leads to *multimedia* that the user can watch and interact with.
- Store menu option at the top – this button leads to https://store.tdjakes.org the online store for The Potter's House where there are numerous *products* offered and is another great website the church has created.

And we are just getting started. When looking at the TPHD website, it definitely provides solutions via products, content *and* multimedia.

That covers the design criteria for the TPHD site. Let's take a look at how it stacks up to the three objectives a church website should meet.

Help People Find a Church to Attend (in person or online) - No problems here. There are two buttons that focus on this; the first is the "Other Locations", which provides the numerous Potter's House Church locations in addition to Dallas in case people want to come to church. The second button that focuses on this is the "Watch Live Now" and this lets people watch online services and attend church from wherever they are via their computer or mobile device.

Inform Church Members of the Current Ministries and Activities – The top menu has two ministry options, local and national. The local button goes to a page that focuses on the local church outreach programs and ministries that a person can join. The national button goes to a page that focuses on the national ministry programs such as conferences, missions and other major outreach initiatives that a person can support. A church member has many options to find something that interests them.

Provide Spiritual Content That Helps People Grow - Again, this is a no-brainer. The "Self Help Section" provides an abundance of spiritual content and focuses on topics that will help build people up, educate them and equip them to overcome issues. Additionally, the products that the online store offers provide hundreds of teachings by Bishop T.D. Jakes on a variety of topics. There may be more items on the site but we would have to click on some links to explore. And that's not a bad thing, is it?

In summary, The Potter's House of Dallas website is pleasing to the eye and easy to use. No user looking at this site should be turned off by anything. It must be working because this church has multiple locations in addition to its amazing online internet church website. That's building the Kingdom! Now, let's focus on your church or ministry's website.

What Components Should Your Church Website Have?

Eye-Catching Color Scheme - Developing an elegant, professional color scheme for your church website is critical. How can you accomplish this? First, look at dozens of websites and find ones with color schemes you like. Narrow the list down to three favorites. Then, have your designer try the colors with your site layout and see how it looks. Next, consider the local colors of your community. What colors are big in your area? Are there some colors that are frowned upon? At some college towns you will not see businesses using the colors of their main rivals. Be careful. Third, select colors that will bring out the look and feel of your church. Consider the age and design of your building. What are the colors on the outside of your church? Is there a consistent color inside your church that you would like to pick up? Fourth, think about who you want to attract. If your church is trying to appeal to 20-somethings and is located in an eclectic area, you can try some vibrant colors. For older members, try traditional browns, grays and dark blues. Fifth, moderation is usually the key to a good color scheme. You do not need eight different colors. Pick a main color and contrast it with a color that works. For example, orange is not easy to contrast with yellow. But orange may work well with a shade of brown. If you are color-challenged, get help. If you are not sure you're color-challenged, get help. Above all, get the color right! Finally, and most important, make sure the website maintains a professional look to it. We all appreciate the hard work volunteers can do on a church website especially if the volunteer just learned how to make websites. But when it comes to an iChurch experience and advancing the Kingdom online, you need to showcase a website of excellence. Remember, the colors you choose will show up on shirt logos, marketing materials and church bulletins. Take your time and get the color right. Here are some good examples of eye-catching color schemes:

- http://www.fellowshipchurch.com/
- http://www.saddleback.com/

Optimized Images - How many times have we heard that a picture is worth a thousand words? Well, for church websites that statement is true. It might also be worth a thousand more visitors or a thousand dollars more in offerings each week. When a website has vibrant images, the user is captivated and stays longer searching the site. They are pulled into the iChurch experience. But what images are best? There are several choices. Consider a wide banner showing the church members in worship. Perhaps use an image of the pastor. Other images that work are church members performing ministry work, members helping each other, and the church building. Some church websites have images of the pastor's products such as past sermons, books and conferences. To obtain first class images, consider a professional photographer. No matter how you obtain the image, make sure you have the copyrights or permission to use the photo on your website. Talk to the person who took the photo and see if they will give you written permission to use the photo. With a dazzling image, your church website will keep visitors coming back. In case your ministry doesn't have any photos

you can purchase royalty free, optimized images for your website from
http://www.istockphoto.com/.

User Interaction - Creating ways to interact with your church website is one of the best ways to engage users. There are a variety of ways to accomplish this:

Online Registration Forms - Not only will this form gather data for later use but registering for church events and activities will be considerably easier for ministry members and visitors.

Online Ministry Forms - This form will save printing costs as members will download and print out the forms, then return them.

Online Donations Modules - One of the most mutually beneficial advancements of technology allows your church website to accept online donations. An online donation is a very convenient way for a member to financially support the ministry and for the ministry to receive the financial support. Online donations can be set up as an immediate transaction or completed at timed intervals such as monthly or annually. Online donation modules using Paypal are shown in the tech talk section of Part 3.

Online Event Calendar - The best way for online users to keep up with the numerous events that occur within the ministry is to have an online event calendar. This calendar can inform users of events as well as let them RSVP and confirm their attendance/participation at an event. Using software such as Google Calendar (http://www.google.com/calendar), a ministry can setup a calendar that online users can interact with and stay informed of ministry events and activities.

Online Prayer Requests - Teaching people how to pray, helping them pray and praying for them is one of the most important foundational activities of a church. Online prayer requests provide users with an easy and effective way to submit prayers to the ministry and become more connected. Users can submit prayers from anywhere and get an automated or customized response that shows their prayer was received and that the ministry will address it.

Multimedia - Both audio and video have completely enhanced the web viewing experience. Your church website should make use of both.

Digital Audio - This can be downloaded or released as a podcast via iTunes. Your church should use digital audio as a way to let online users download sermons. You can also release the sermons to iTunes as a podcast (we will discuss this below). This can all be done for free or a minimal cost.

Digital Video - Users can watch archived sermons in video or watch live streaming sermons as they happen. You may want to allow the user to download a video of past sermons which they can share via social networking sites. Digital Videos should be prominently placed on the homepage as well as located in a section where users can easily access it. Using video sharing sites such as YouTube.com and Vimeo.com are low cost and free solutions in giving your users a great a digital video experience.

Content Management System (CMS) - If your site has numerous pages and collects information from a variety of ministries and internal departments, a CMS is a must. It allows non-technical users to update their own areas of the website. It also allows the technical staff to manage the website, restrict access and change the look of the website with minimal repetitive work and time.

Site Map - This is a single webpage that has a link to "all" the pages within a website. You may see this at the footer (bottom) of most websites. The rule of thumb for websites is that users should be able to get to all pages within two to three clicks. This could be completed with menus and sub-navigation (subnav) links but the backup plan for this rule is usually the site map. Since online users who come to your website aren't usually familiar with all the pages, a sitemap is a good page to have to help guide them through your site and find the webpage/information they are looking for.

Rotating Banners - These are images that rotate on a timed basis on your website. http://www.tdjakes.org/ provides an excellent example of rotating banners. A church can show multiple images in a short time while the user simply waits for the next image to come up. Rotating banners give you the ability to inform the online user about current events, books to buy, donations needed and upcoming events. These banners really catch the attention of online users and can effectively engage and hold the user on your site.

New Visitor Link - The majority of new users to a church's website are not familiar with the church prior to coming there. They may be familiar with the pastor from watching him on television or seeing him at a conference but they may not see the website in the same way a familiar church member may see it. The best item to have on a church website is a button or link that says "I'm New to [church name here]" or "New Visitors Click Here." When a new online user clicks this link, your website should provide information about your church, your beliefs, service times, current events and activities, the leadership of the church and possibly introduce them to your church with a video. This page is where your church puts its best foot forward and says to possible visitors, "We would love to have you come visit our church!"

Social Media Icons - Social media icons are the small colorful symbols you see at the bottom of most websites. Facebook uses a lowercase f in a blue background square. Twitter uses a lowercase t in a light blue background square. Each of the icons has a link embedded in them that allow the online user to click on it and arrive at the social media page for the website owner. These icons are usually in a highly visible area such as the header or footer.

Visual Icon Menu - The visual icon menu is usually a horizontal display of icons that allow the online user to obtain more information about the church. Instead of tabs, these icons allow for a more visually pleasing display of things the users may be looking for. See http://www.tdjakes.org/ and look halfway down for the words "I want to connect." Then follow the list horizontally for a good example of a visual icon menu.

Newsletter Registration - If you have a newsletter, having an online registration form is a must. The form can be a button or link that the online user clicks on that takes the user to a set of questions and allows him to quickly sign up for the newsletter. An online newsletter registration form allows users a way to stay connected to the ministry without having to come to the website. This also gives the ministry a way to reach the online users with content, products, updates and other marketing messages.

Website Analytics - How many visitors does your website receive each day? Which pages do they visit? How long do they stay? Web analytics answers these questions. It is like having someone tell you how close your ball is on the green after you have hit it from the fairway. With information from web analytics, you can make adjustments on your site and improve the user's experience. Web analytics can be obtained for free by using software such as Google Analytics (http://www.google.com/analytics).

High Quality Content - Have you ever read a website that had poor grammar or bad spelling? Maybe the sentence structure was obtuse. Do you even know what "obtuse" means? Chances are your website users won't. For all websites, there is a very common saying: content is king. Your church website needs intriguing and easy-to-understand content.

Where do you find this content? There are numerous sources that can be used for the church's website. First and foremost, there should be content on the beliefs, mission and vision of the church. Also, topical content on hot button topics that ministry members need to know such as God, Life, Family, Work, Finances, Health, Marriage, and Relationships should be included. There needs to be content on the church, its ministries and its current events. Other content topics include information about spiritual perspectives and ministry opportunities. Some of this content should be in the form of multimedia video and audio. It should engage the users and inform them visually as well as audibly.

The easiest way to generate content is to *repurpose* the content that is created by the pastor. Each week, the pastor delivers a message of new content. This content can be packaged and delivered (repurposed) in a variety of ways to online users.

- The pastor's message can be re-distributed by media through the mail.
- It can be printed in periodicals and publications.
- It can be offered in a media player on a website.
- It can become part of a podcast, updated weekly with very little effort or financial cost.

- Pieces of that message can become blog posts when re-worked for an online reading audience.
- More pieces can be sent out by email as a daily devotional.
- Nuggets from that message can be tweeted and retweeted, or shared on Facebook.
- A short clip from the message (if recorded on video) can be uploaded to YouTube.
- A slideshow from the message can be shared online.
- The message can be turned into a CD or DVD for purchase.
- The message(s) can be transformed into a book or ebook.
- The message can be turned into a mp3 (audio) or mp4 (video) digital download.

While this is not quite as good as turning fives loaves and two fish into a meal that fed a multitude, it's a close second. One message equals twelve content possibilities. Repurposing allows us to be good stewards of the pastor's skill, education and hard work. Imagine how fast Christianity would have spread if within hours of the him speaking the words, Jesus' sermon on the mount reached out though Facebook, Twitter and YouTube? We should make sure we take the content that is already available to us (five loaves and two fish) and put it to its fullest possible use, spreading it around the website in a variety of manners. As long your website is full of great spiritual content and it's continually updated and refreshed, online users will continue to return and consume it. One final thought, having *high quality content* is a necessity even if you have to pay for it.

What I Want For My iChurch - Part 1

(a) I need a website.

(b) Objectives for my website (highlight the ones you want):

    1. Help people find a church to attend.

    2. Inform potential and active church members of the current ministries and events.

    3. Provide spiritual content that helps people grow in their faith.

4. Provide information about the need for ministry work in _____.

5. Explain what the ministry is currently doing in _____.

6. Request donations through an online payment system.

7. Sell products.

(c) Design Criteria for my website (highlight the ones you want):

1. Clean or uncluttered (not busy).

2. Informative by providing helpful content.

3. Cause the user to interact with the website.

4. Engaging and interesting.

5. Provide solutions via products, content and/or multimedia.

(d) Things I want on my website (button or tab or link somewhere on the website).

1. New Visitors.

2. View messages or sermons.

3. A map or directions how to get to my church.

4. Our different locations.

5. Our Vision.

6. Our Mission Statement

7. Our Values.

8. I Need Help - where the online user can get help for a variety of problems in their life.

9. Quality Images of (select one or more) our pastor, church, congregation, ministry.

10. Eye-Catching color scheme. Try the following colors _____.

11. Podcasts to download.

12. eBooks to download.

13. Steps to become a member.

14. Login for current members.

15. Newsletter and Newsletter Registration.

16. Online Registration Forms.

17. Online Ministry Forms.

18. Online Donations Modules.

19. Online Event Calendar.

20. Online Prayer Requests.

21. Content Management System.

22. Site Map.

23. Website Analytics.

24. Blog.

25. Daily devotional.

26. Facebook page and link.

27. Twitter account and link.

28. Bible link.

29. Navigation Menu.

30. History of our Church.

31. Contact Us.

32. Copyright logo and date.

33. Rotating Banners.

34. Social Media Icons

35. Visual Icon Menu

Let's Talk Tech

Now let's break down the layout of a popular ministry website that I have worked on. This site is located at tdjakes.org. I will take the code that is available via the <u>View Source Code</u> option and break it down to explain how the page was put together.

The above website is http://www.tdjakes.org in 2011. I worked on this website redesign during the Fall of 2010 because we were looking to create a great website that exemplified Bishop T.D. Jakes online. This website was created by professional designer Joseph Anthony (@josephanthony4) and put into Adobe Photoshop PSD format. From there, the developers took the design and with photoshop, sliced it up into images that were used to create this webpage. Here are the parts that make this website a great online presence:

1. Top Navigation menu - The top navigation menu is where you include the logo and the main webpages on the website. This menu appears on all pages. Thus it needs to focus on the main areas of the website as well as help direct online users to the areas that they want to visit quickly and most often. On a church website, we see that the main areas are the *about* section explaining the beliefs of the ministry, the *online store* displaying products for easy purchasing, the *TV section* for a ministry that has a large television following, a *link to the actual church* if the ministry is connected to a church, the *contact us* section to give ministry supporters and online users an easy way to reach out to the ministry and finally, the *donations* sections to provide a smooth and simple online way for users to financially support the ministry. The top menu is simply a navigation menu image from the PSD that was sliced into a jpg. format, put into an image map and the links were added via hotspots.

<img src="images/top2new.jpg" width="1200" border="0" usemap="#m_imagemap">

```
<map name="m_imagemap" id="m_imagemap">
<area shape="rect" coords="935,77,1038,99" href="http://www.tdjakes.org/contact.html" title="Contact Us" alt="Contact Us" />
<area shape="rect" coords="753,76,910,98" href="http://www.thepottershouse.org" target="_blank" title="The Potter's House" alt="The Potter's House" />
<area shape="rect" coords="1066,73,1205,116" href="https://store.tdjakes.org/donation.aspx" target="_blank" title="Donations" alt="Donations" />
<area shape="rect" coords="501,76,556,100" href="https://store.tdjakes.org/" target="_blank" title="Online Store" alt="Online Store" /> <area shape="rect" coords="66,14,255,107" href="http://www.tdjakes.org" title="tdjakes.org" alt="tdjakes.org" /> <area shape="rect" coords="393,76,473,100" href="http://www.tdjakes.org/itinerary.html" target="_blank" title="Itinerary" alt="Itinerary" />
<area shape="rect" coords="309,75,367,100" href="http://www.tdjakes.org/about.html" title="About" alt="About" /> <area shape="rect" coords="582,77,726,99" href="http://www.tdjakes.org/prayer.html" target="_blank" title="featured Product" alt="featured product">
</map>
```

2. Rotating Banners - Just a few years back, rotating banners were done in flash. But as of the last few years, rotating banners are now done in JQuery. JQuery is a mixture of JavaScript and CSS and it is mobile website friendly so the website you create can be viewed on mobile devices as well. If you are not a programmer, you can get the code from http://jqueryui.com. Rotating banners are large graphics that are utilized to catch the online users attention as soon as they enter the website. These can be just visual images or they can be "clickable" banner links to subpages or other websites.

```html
<link href="newbanner/Slideshow.css" type="text/css" rel="stylesheet" />
<script src="newbanner/jQuery.js" type="text/javascript"></script> <script
src="newbanner/Slideshow.js" type="text/javascript" charset="utf-8"></script>
<link href="newbanner/style.css" rel="stylesheet" type="text/css" />


<div id=tmpSlideshow>
<div class='tmpSlide' id='tmpSlide-1'><a href='http://tdjakes.org/August2011'
target='_blank'><img src='images/banner_divinestrategies1000.jpg' border='0'
/></a></div>

<div class='tmpSlide' id='tmpSlide-2'><a href='http://www.manpowerconference.org'
target='_blank'><img src='images/banner_mp_ipad_hemotions.jpg' border='0'
/></a></div>

<div class='tmpSlide' id='tmpSlide-3'><a href='http://tdjakes.org/thecrossing'
target='_blank'><img src='images/banner_thecrossing1000.jpg' border='0' /></a></div>

<div class='tmpSlide' id='tmpSlide-4'><a href='http://www.wtal.org'
target='_blank'><img src='images/banner_wtal1000.jpg' border='0' /></a></div>

<div class='tmpSlide' id='tmpSlide-5'><a
href='http://www.tdjakes.org/sacredlovesongs2/' target='_blank'><img
src='images/banner_sacredlovesongs1000.jpg' border='0' /></a></div>

<div class='tmpSlide' id='tmpSlide-6'><a href='http://www.tdjpartners.org/'
target='_blank'><img src='images/banner-partner.jpg' border='0' /></a></div>

<div id="tmpSlideshowControls">
<div class='tmpSlideshowControl'id='tmpSlideshowControl-1'><img
src='images/bluedot.jpg' /></div>
<div class='tmpSlideshowControl'id='tmpSlideshowControl-2'><img
src='images/bluedot.jpg' /></div>
```

```
<div class='tmpSlideshowControl'id='tmpSlideshowControl-3'><img
src='images/bluedot.jpg' /></div>
<div class='tmpSlideshowControl'id='tmpSlideshowControl-4'><img
src='images/bluedot.jpg' /></div>
<div class='tmpSlideshowControl'id='tmpSlideshowControl-5'><img
src='images/bluedot.jpg' /></div>
<div class='tmpSlideshowControl'id='tmpSlideshowControl-6'><img
src='images/bluedot.jpg' /></div>
</div>
```

3. Social Media Icons - Social media icons need to be prevalent on your church website. Usually in a highly visible area such as the header or footer. Simply use the facebook, youtube and twitter icons in jpg. or png. format and make them links to your social media webpages. You can grab the icons from google.com. Go to google and do a search for facebook, then copy a facebook icon to use, and then do the same for twitter and youtube. When you put these icons on your website, you want to link them to your ministry's facebook, twitter and youtube pages. We discuss how to create these pages in Part 4, Social Media.

4. Multimedia Videos - Multimedia videos are one of the best ways to enhance your church website. You need to have your videos made into web-ready format and to complete this you need to load them up to a web video provider such as youtube.com, vimeo.com or a custom software provider. Vimeo.com is my video provider of choice. On this webpage we took vimeo web code (explained below in Phase 2 multimedia) and put it into a JQuery Carousel. The code for a JQuery Carousel is located here http://sorgalla.com/projects/jcarousel. Here, the example uses images but you simply replace the image code <img src=....> with code for the vimeo video <iframe src=""...></iframe>.

```
<script type="text/javascript" src="newbanner/lib/jquery.jcarousel.min.js"></script>
```

```
<iframe src="rotatevids.html" name="videorow" width="1010" height="305"
frameborder="0" marginheight="0" marginwidth="0" style="background-color:#fff"
scrolling="no"></iframe>
```

Rotatevids.html

```
<ul id="mycarousel" class="jcarousel-skin-tango">
  <!-- Pastors and Leaders --><li><div style="text-align:center;"><strong>2012 Pastors
and Leaders</strong></div><iframe
src="http://player.vimeo.com/video/35589223?title=0&amp;byline=0&amp;portrait=0&a
mp;color=000000" width="300" height="245" frameborder="0"></iframe>
</li>


  <!-- The Potter's Touch--><li><div align="center"><strong>The Potter's Touch
Broadcast</strong></div><iframe
src="http://player.vimeo.com/video/17196609?title=0&amp;byline=0&amp;portrait=0"
width="300" height="245" frameborder="0"></iframe>
</li>


  <!--Let it Go--><li><div align="center"><strong>Let it Go</strong></div>
<iframe
src="http://player.vimeo.com/video/34540995?title=0&amp;byline=0&amp;portrait=0&a
mp;color=000000" width="300" height="245" frameborder="0"></iframe>
</li>


  <!--Satellite Churches <li> <div align="center"><strong>TPH Satellite Church
Pastors</strong></div> <iframe
src="http://player.vimeo.com/video/18553473?title=0&amp;byline=0&amp;portrait=0&a
mp;color=000000" width="300" height="245" frameborder="0"></iframe> </li>-->


  <!--TDJ Social Media--> <li><div align="center"><strong>TDJ Social
Media</strong></div> <iframe
src="http://player.vimeo.com/video/17196334?title=0&amp;byline=0&amp;portrait=0"
width="300" height="245" frameborder="0"></iframe> </li>


  <!-- We Are the Potters House -->
<li><div align="center"><strong>We Are the Potter's House</strong></div> <iframe
src="http://player.vimeo.com/video/17196349?title=0&amp;byline=0&amp;portrait=0"
width="300" height="245" frameborder="0"></iframe> </li>
```

5. Visual icon menu - The visual icon menu is where we visually guide the online users. The title at the top of the menu is "I want to connect." Here, the website is letting the online users that want to connect to the ministry know where they can find the things they are looking for. The visual icon menu has quite a few items from the main navigation menu but also adds in multimedia links such as "watch live" and "instant inspiration". "Watch live" is a link to the live streaming service and "instant inspiration" is a link to the online media player. To create this menu we use the same technique as the top navigation menu, a menu image from the PSD that was sliced into a jpg, put into an image map and the links were added via hotspots.

6. Newsletter registration - Every webpage, ministry or business, should have a newsletter registration button or form. This gives users a way to stay connected to the ministry without having to come to the website. This also gives the ministry a way to reach the online users with content, products, updates and other marketing messages. The newsletter is named "Become an Insider" because it gives a feeling of exclusivity and exception to the average online user. The "insider" gets access to exclusive information and products that the average user may not and that is always a benefit. This link is simply an image that links to a newsletter sign up webpage. The easiest way to setup a newsletter signup page is to use a service such as aweber.com or constantcontact.com. These services help you setup newsletter lists as well as give you the code to create newsletter sign up webpages. Once you get that code and create that page, you can link it to the image above and you have your newsletter registration.

7. Footer - The footer of the church website is simply a recap of what the website is about and a few important links. There is the copyright information, possibly a logo again, and a footer menu that has the important links that online users may have missed higher on the page. Since the footer appears on all pages in the website, it is an important part of the website. To create this footer we use the same technique as the top navigation menu, a menu image from the PSD that was sliced into a jpg. then put into an image map where the links were added via hotspots.

```
<img src="images/bottom1.jpg" width="1200" border="0" usemap="#m_bottommap">

<map name="m_bottommap" id="m_bottommap">
<area shape="rect" coords="1024,23,1090,37" href="http://www.tdjakes.org/mobile/">

<area shape="rect" coords="1096,23,1166,39"
href="http://www.tdjakes.org/contact.html" alt="">
```

```html
<area shape="rect" coords="900,24,1017,39" href="http://thepottershouse.org"
target="_blank" title="The Potter's House" alt="The Potter's House" />
<area shape="rect" coords="830,23,901,40"
href="https://store.tdjakes.org/donation.aspx" target="_blank" title="Donations"
alt="Donations" />
<area shape="rect" coords="793,23,835,39" href="https://store.tdjakes.org/"
target="_blank" title="Online Store" alt="Online Store" />
<area shape="rect" coords="735,23,791,39"
href="http://www.thepottershouse.org/Local/Events-and-Calendar/Bishops-
Itinerary.aspx" target="_blank" title="Bishop's Itinerary" alt="Bishop's Itinerary" />
<area shape="rect" coords="690,23,735,38" href="http://www.tdjakes.org/about.html"
title="About" alt="About" />  <area shape="rect" coords="646,23,692,39"
href="http://www.tdjakes.org" target="_self" title="tdjakes.org" alt="Home" />
</map>
```

Sidenote: This page has an image background where the grey fades from dark grey to white. The top of the page background is dark grey and as you get further down the page it fades to white. Here is the code that made that possible.

```html
<body bgcolor="#FFFFFF" leftmargin="0" topmargin="0" marginwidth="0"
marginheight="0" style="background: url('images/bg.jpg') repeat-x" >
```

The above webpage is a subpage from http://www.tdjakes.org, more specifically it's the *itinerary page*. The subpages are very similar to the homepage but there are some differences that set them apart from the homepage. The subpages are created for easy content display as well as quick page duplication. Normally there are numerous subpages on a website therefore the design of a subpage has to be similar to other subpages with a few changes such as left navigation menus, content and subpage banners. I explain further below.

1. Top Navigation menu – same as the previous page.

2. Subpage banner - The subpage banner is a large image that showcases what the current webpage is about. Since online users may visit a variety of subpages, the subpage banner is usually the first image they see on the page and its main focus is to visually convey to online users what the focus of this subpage is about. The banner on this page is the title Bishop's Calendar with a date book next to it.

3. Left navigation menu - To create the left navigation menu, we took the visual icon menu and had the graphic artist recreate it as a left navigation menu to appear on the left side of pages instead of the bottom. For this website we used a two column div where the left side was the left navigation menu and the right side was the content. Within the left side <div> the left navigation menu is an image from the PSD that was sliced into a jpg. then put into an image map with the links added via hotspots.

4. Content Section - The content section on a subpage is a designated area that has content on all the subpages. For this website we used a two column div where the left side was the left navigation menu and the right side was the content. Within the right side <div> has the content which is set at a width of 700 pixels, justified paragraphs and HTML code. The code is below.

```
<div align="left" style="width:700px; text-align:justify; margin-top:300px; padding-left:10px;"><p><strong><u><span style="font-size: 18pt"> MARCH</span></u></strong><br><p><br><strong>&quot;Let It Go&quot; Speaking Tour<br>March 4, 2012</strong><br>7:00 pm<br>Worship Service <br>Bishop Charles Blake<br>West Angeles Church of God in Christ<br>3600 Crenshaw Blvd.<br>Los Angeles, CA 90016<br>323-733-8300 or <a href="http://www.westa.org/" target="_blank">www.westa.org</a></p>
```

5. Footer - same as the previous page.

How to setup a Website with a CMS

Let's look at a simple way to setup a website for a ministry. There are a few free/low-cost tools out there that will provide great websites. Here are two that I am aware of are:

- http://www.coffeecup.com
- http://www.google.com/sites/help/intl/en/overview.html

Both of these website editors provide users, whether they are technical or novices, with the tools to create a high quality, great looking website. If a ministry needs to create a website and does not have any technical people on staff, I would suggest using one of these. On the other hand, if you do have a technical person on staff, I suggest that you use wordpress to setup a website by using the following steps below.

How to setup a Wordpress website.

Here is a quick snapshot of the steps it takes to create a Wordpress CMS website on Godaddy.

1. Get domain and hosting from Godaddy.com.
2. Setup FTP login for ftp user access.
3. Install Wordpress on Godaddy.
4. Install template.
5. Start creating pages.

Now let's explain how to setup a wordpress website with a few more details.

1. **Get a domain and hosting from Godaddy.com** - Purchase a domain and hosting from Godaddy.com. Godaddy.com is one of numerous web domain and hosting providers available, and I have found that in working with many of them, Godaddy.com has the easiest process to purchase domains, setup hosting and get a website up quickly.

2. **Setup FTP login for user access** – once you have purchased and setup your domain, you can now access your hosting account from your godaddy login. To do this you need to login into Godaddy.com and then click on **A. My Account**. Once you click on my account you should get a screen that looks like the one

below. Then Click in the B section where it has a **--Web Hosting** – tab and click on the name of your hosting account to launch (if this is your first time clicking on it then you will need to set it up, which is a few more clicks).

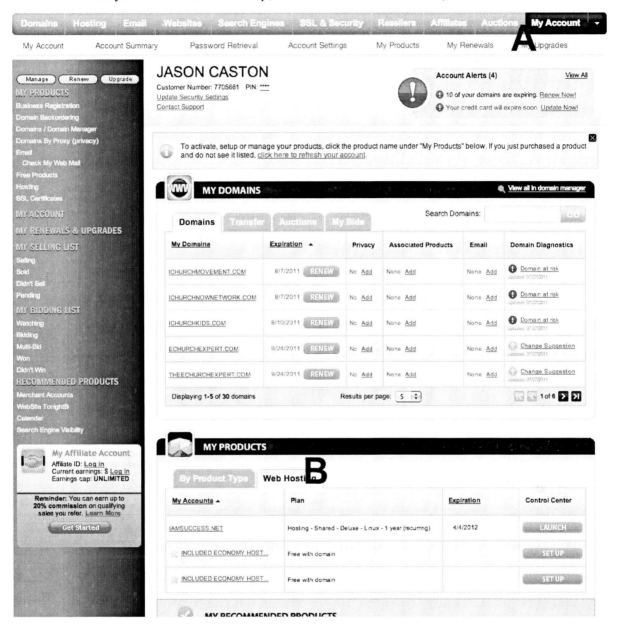

Once you launch the hosting, you will then see the following screen. Here you want to setup your FTP login. FTP is short for **- - File Transfer Protocol - -** which is simply the way you upload files to your website server. Click on **A. FTP Users** to setup your FTP account.

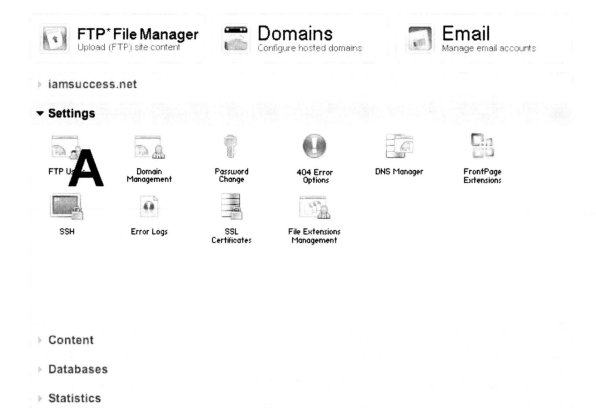

Next step is to setup the username and password for your ftp account. Choose something that you will remember but that no one else can guess. We don't want your account to get hacked. Once you have completed this step, you are ready to install Wordpress.

FTP Users

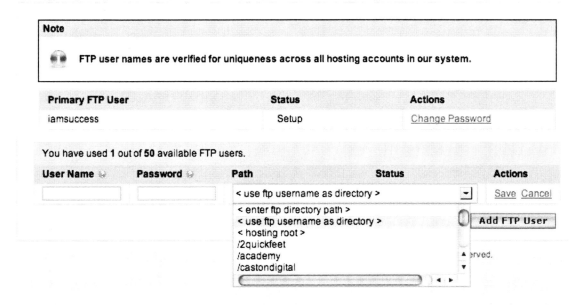

3. **Install Wordpress on Godaddy** – Click on the home tab at the top of the page (not pictured) to get back to the main hosting page. On the right you should see an - - **Applications** - - button which is what you want to click next. That will take you to the applications homepage where you will install and setup your Wordpress software.

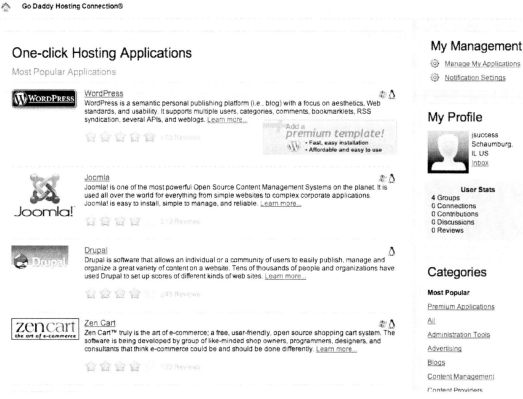

If you don't see Wordpress as one of the application options, type Wordpress into the search field and click the yellow search button. Once you see Wordpress, click on the Wordpress title to get to the installation page.

WordPress 3.2.1 Installation

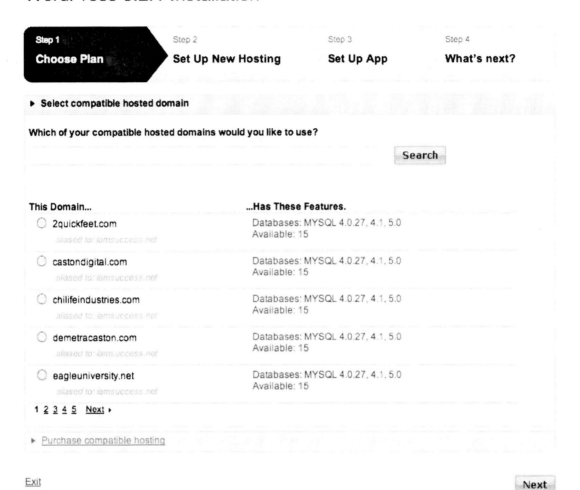

Step 1	Step 2	Step 3	Step 4
Choose Plan	**Set Up New Hosting**	**Set Up App**	**What's next?**

▶ **Select compatible hosted domain**

Which of your compatible hosted domains would you like to use?

[   ] [Search]

This Domain...	...Has These Features.
○ 2quickfeet.com *aliased to: iamsuccess.net*	Databases: MYSQL 4.0.27, 4.1, 5.0 Available: 15
○ castondigital.com *aliased to: iamsuccess.net*	Databases: MYSQL 4.0.27, 4.1, 5.0 Available: 15
○ chilifeindustries.com *aliased to: iamsuccess.net*	Databases: MYSQL 4.0.27, 4.1, 5.0 Available: 15
○ demetracaston.com *aliased to: iamsuccess.net*	Databases: MYSQL 4.0.27, 4.1, 5.0 Available: 15
○ eagleuniversity.net *aliased to: iamsuccess.net*	Databases: MYSQL 4.0.27, 4.1, 5.0 Available: 15

1 2 3 4 5 Next ▶

▶ Purchase compatible hosting

Exit   [Next]

First step is to choose which domain you are going to use for this installation. (Note that this is the Wordpress 3.2.1, that is the current version at the time of this book, December 2010, you may have a more updated version when you are installing Wordpress). There should only be one domain if this is your first godaddy account and Wordpress installation. Once you are done, click the yellow Next button.

WordPress 3.2.1 Installation

Step 1	Step 2	Step 3	Step 4
Choose Plan	**Set Up New Hosting**	**Set Up App**	**What's next?**

Domain: demetracaston.com | *Aliased To:* iamsuccess.net/demetra

▶ **Set up database**

Database/User Name: dem1121808573808

Database description:

WordPress

Example: "Database for WordPress 3.2.1 on demetracaston.com"

Create a database password:

•••••••••

Verify password:

••••••••••

You will need this password to make changes to the database later.

`Next`

▶ Choose install directory

▶ Configuration

◂ Back to "Choose Domain"

The next step is to choose the name of your Wordpress database (which can just be Wordpress) and then a password. Once you are done, click the yellow Next button.

WordPress 3.2.1 Installation

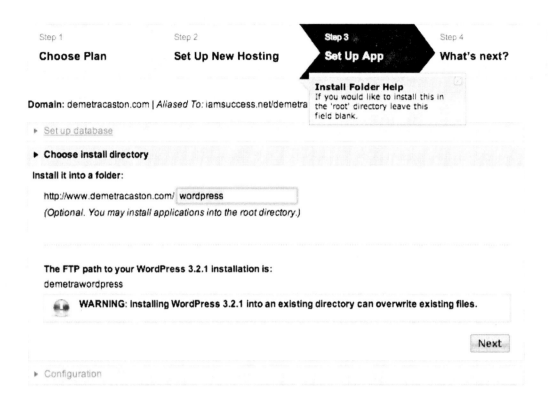

The last few steps are to choose which folder/directory Wordpress will be installed to. You can either leave it as Wordpress or change it to a name that you desire. If you don't want to use any folders or directories, then delete the name and leave it blank and you will install it into the root directory. Once you click the yellow Next button, you will then choose your username and password for Wordpress and the installation will begin. The installation should take anywhere between 4 – 24 hours. Once that is complete, you can login to wordpress at http://www.yourchurchwebsite.com/wp-admin/.

4. **Install Web Layout Template** – Now that you have Wordpress installed on your webserver, you need to install a template that fits the design layout for your ministry. To install a template, click on the **- - Appearance - -** tab in the left column.

Once you click on Appearance you will then come to the page below. Then you will click on – **Install Themes** – which should take you to the installation page. Once on the installation page, you will click on - - **Upload** - - and that will give you the option to upload a theme you have saved. If you do not have a theme saved then you can search through the theme gallery that Wordpress has available.

Dashboard

Jetpack

Posts

Media

Links

Pages

Comments

iBlogPro

Theme Options

Feature Setup

Appearance

Themes

Widgets

Menus

Editor

Plugins

Users

Tools

Settings

General

Writing

Reading

Discussion

Media

Privacy

Permalinks

CMS Tree Page View

Collapse menu

SVTX Church

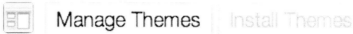 Manage Themes   Install Themes

Jetpack is installed and ready to bring aweso

Learn More

Current Theme

iBlogPro 4.2.6 by PageLines

iBlogPro is a professional WordPress then

OPTIONS: Widgets I Menus

Available Themes

Twenty Eleven 1.2 by the WordPress team

The 2011 theme for WordPress is sophisticated, lightweight, and adaptable. Make it yours with a custom menu, header image, and background — then go further with available theme options for light or dark color scheme, custom link colors, and three layout choices. Twenty Eleven comes equipped with a Showcase page template that transforms your front page into a showcase to show

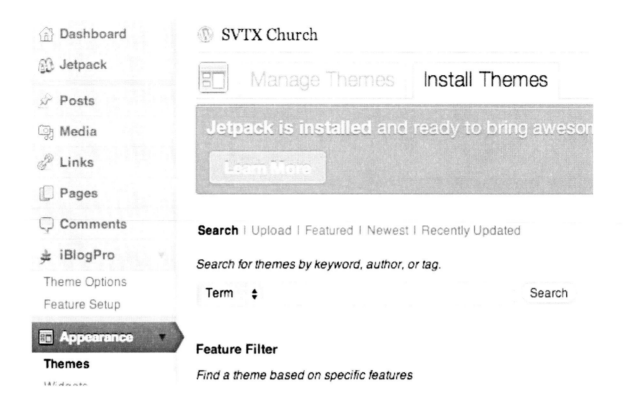

5. **Start creating pages** – Now that we have the template installed and the look of your new ministry website is starting to come together, we need to start creating pages with content on them. Click on pages in the left menu and then at the top of the page click on - - **Add New** – to create a new page.

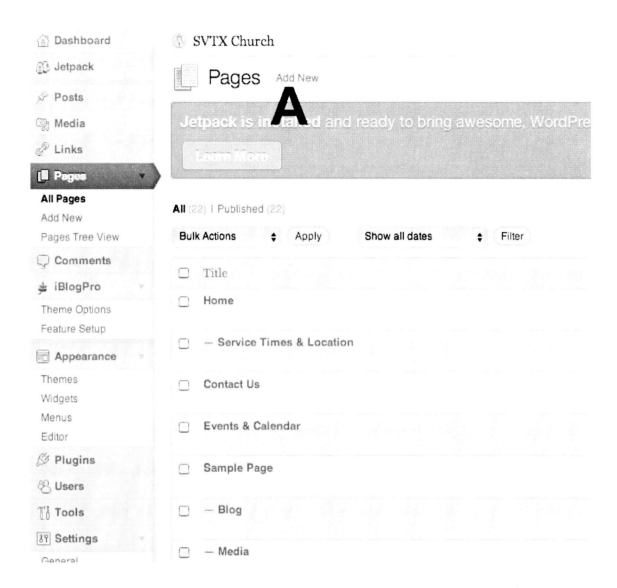

Once you add the content for your page, you can click - - **Publish** - - on the right hand side and you will have a page for your website. Now there's one more thing you need to do to make sure online users can get to your newly created pages. Pages that are created are not automatically added to the menus of the website. You have to manually go in and add them to the menu. To do this, you can click on - - **Menus** - - under - - **Appearance** - - on the left column. When you click on **Menu** you will get the page below. Once you choose which pages you want to add to the menu (there should be only one page in the - - **Pages** - - box on the left side), you can then click on the - - **Save Menu** - - button on the right and you are good to go.

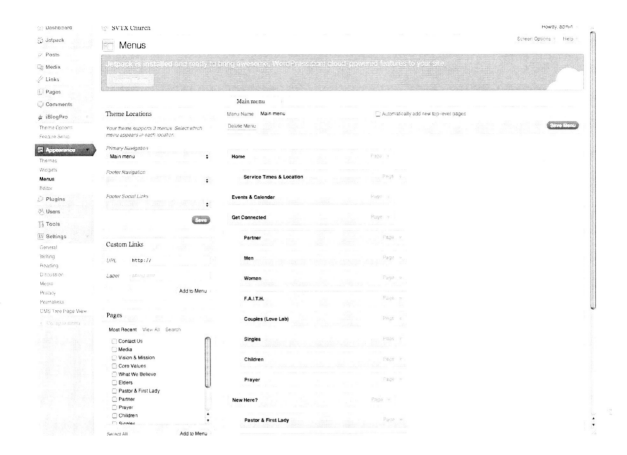

Part 2
Interactive Multimedia

Let's Talk Strategy

What is Multimedia?

Multimedia is multiple types of media. *Media* is the plural form of the word medium. *Medium* is a way to communicate content (i.e., "television is a powerful *medium*"). Essentially, multimedia means *multiple types of ways to communicate content.* That's a mouthful. So what does all that mean? Here's a brief explanation.

When the first website arrived, it was primitive; words on a screen. If the writer was looking at a beautiful rose, the best he could do for the user was to write a description of the rose and type the words onto the web page. That was it. The rose, in this example, is the *content.* The writer's description of the rose in the form of words on the screen is the delivery method or *medium.* Simple.

As technology advanced, the writer could upload a still photo of the rose to his website for the online user to view. The content was still the rose yet the delivery method was via a still image (another medium). As time moved on, technology allowed a video (yet another medium) of this same rose. Also, audio could accompany the video. And audio could be separated out from the video allowing the online user to hear only the audio (again, another medium). Thus, through documents, images, video and audio, content could be delivered in multiple ways.

Yet the first delivery methods required the online user to be chained to their computer and monitor. Technology soon provided a solution: an online user could download the content to their iPod, iPad, smart phone, laptop or similar device and carry it away from their computer to view in a park, listen while working out or read during a lunch break. This created a form of portable multimedia. Today, portable devices expand multimedia by allowing an online user to view content anywhere, anytime. So how does this term *Multimedia* affect the iChurch and apply to your ministry?

Think about it. You can simply type words on the screen to deliver the pastor's weekly message. That takes little effort. Or you can take photos of the pastor at the pulpit and place the still images along with the typed words. Or you can take a copy of the video from last Sunday's sermon and allow the online user to watch it anytime, day or night. Or you can set up a live streaming video for the online user to watch in real-time. That's very first-class. And all of the above are examples of *Multimedia*: delivering content in a variety of ways to the end user. Simple.

Let's look at each delivery method and see how you can fully use Multimedia for the iChurch.

Video

Website visitors and consumers love to watch videos. Given a choice, a person will choose watching a video over reading text. Because of this, the iChurch must take advantage of the video options available. What are the video options?

- On-Demand Video
- Live Streaming Video
- Podcast

It all begins with a video recording. Let's start with the weekly sermon. When you record the pastor's sermon, you can record it with a digital recorder such as a Canon professional video camera or a Flip camera. This digital recorder will record both audio and video. The simplest form of an iChurch video is a single video camera. Some churches have multiple cameras. Others have a separate audio feed. Regardless of what your church has, recording as much of the service as possible is a must.

You will record it in a particular digital format. The most used and current video formats are:

- **mp4** - This is a common format that is used by numerous developers and industries. It has a very good compression for internet streaming and digital distribution (uses the mpeg4 encoder).

- **mov** - This is a similar format to mp4 but is not as common and does not compress as well. But it is still a good format to use.

- **m4v** - This is a common format that has been utilized mostly by Apple. It uses the mpeg4 encoder similar to mp4 and has good compression for smaller file sizes but still maintains high quality video and audio.

- **wmv** - This is Microsoft's video format for Windows videos. The compression is very good and creates very small files with great quality audio and video. The drawback is that to play these videos on Macs, you need an add on (flip4mac) within Quicktime.

Geek Tip: What is all this talk about *compression*? If you have ever seen a nozzle shoved into a plastic sweater package where the air is sucked out (shrink-wrapped), then you can understand the concept of compression. Since video, audio and still images are turned into data, a file is nothing but a ton of squares with numbers in them. Many squares are empty. Compression reads these empty spaces and pushes all the data closer together. Then, the smaller, shrunken file is sent over the internet at a faster speed to your computer which pumps the air back in and expands the file to its original form. The only thing that is different between compressed data and shrink-wrapping a sweater is that when the data is uncompressed or expanded, it is not exactly the way it was originally. But you will not likely be able to see the difference. When you hear the words *good compression*, it means that when the file expands back, it has lost very little content.

Now back to the video options. On-demand video is first.

What is *On-Demand Video*?

When you visit a website and click on a video, you are actually receiving that video to your computer in a stream like water running through a pipe. This is called *on-demand video*. As you watch the video, it is flowing through the pipe to your computer and monitor. When you hit the pause button, the water or video stops streaming. Hit the play button and it starts streaming again. That's all there is to it. You control when it starts and stops. That's the reason it's called "on-demand." This should make the next one easy.

What is *live streaming video*?

You guessed it. The video is streaming to you *live* while it is happening. On Sunday morning, when the pastor starts his sermon, you see it live, just like you were there. Whether you are in China on a trip, at home sick or just want to check out a service before attending in person, you can see the service live without having to show up in person.

Finally, what is a *podcast*?

A podcast is an audio or video file that you can download from a church's website or iTunes and watch on your computer, iPod, iPhone, iPad or other mobile device. As technology has improved, you no longer have to sit chained to your computer waiting for the stream of video to flow. You can now go to a church's website, click on the video link you want to see and download the entire file to your personal computer in a matter of moments. Or you can go to iTunes and search for podcasts and download them from there. Instead of having to wait for the water to come through the pipe, this is like having a 5-gallon bottle of water delivered to your house. Why is this important and newsworthy? It's important because you can take the water or video anywhere with you on your portable device such as an iPod, iPad or laptop computer. Ministry is not limited to only when you are at the computer. You can now take it with you and receive ministry anywhere at any time.

Geek Talk - Where does the word *podcast* come from? Early on this delivery method was called *webcast* like *web broadcast* (i.e., television broadcast). But as soon as the iPod came along and website visitors were allowed to download these big bottles of water or files to their iPod, the word Podcast was born.

Video Uses for iChurch

Now that you know the three delivery methods for video, what are the uses for your iChurch? The obvious one is live streaming video of the sermon each week. Allowing online users to connect with your church live essentially expands your building without having to hire an architect and general contractor. Plus, church members will be able to see your weekly service if they are sick, in the hospital or traveling. Live streaming video is an arrow your iChurch should have in its quiver.

That leaves On-demand videos as the other half of the video coin. Once your church has recorded the live service, it can easily make them available on the website for visitors to access. And remember, this can be set up two ways: On-demand streaming video (where they are watching from their computer or mobile device via a mobile website or app (more about mobile in Part 5)) and podcasts (where they can download it to their computer and/or take it with them on their portable devices). Your iChurch can set up a searchable directory for online users to access. This allows them to search by date or by topic assuming you have labeled each video with topic keywords (which you should do).

But there are many other events and activities a church has besides a sermon. Outreach ministries can easily generate a video to be uploaded to the iChurch. Community activities, church bazaars, sports events and guest speakers are but a few more videos to be recorded and uploaded to the website.

How about taking one video event and multiplying it? *Repurposing* is the answer. Repurposing can take a single video product and turn it into multiple video products. To explain repurposing, let's assume your church has one camera. From this single recording, we can cut up the pastor's thirty-minute message into five-minute segments.

You may find breaking points at different intervals other than five minutes but the point is the single message can be cut up into multiple segments which allow the website visitor to receive the content in a more convenient time-friendly manner. These five-minute segments can be delivered through the church's website and they can be added to a social media network sites like Vimeo, YouTube and Facebook. This gives the user multiple access points to find the pastor's message or content. Think of multiple access points like multiple locations of your church. A franchise creates the same store all over the country. Access points such as the church's website, a Facebook page and a Twitter feed mimic the franchise model. We will discuss all this later in Part 4. The main point you should take from this is that technology allows you to easily create multiple products from one piece of content and this expands the iChurch exponentially!

Another great use of video is children. Studies show that children have become accustomed to multi-sensory stimulation in the development of their learning capabilities. Video has been the leader in this development. How many times have you seen young children glued to the television watching the same video over and over? Now these children have switched to the computer. Why not provide them videos from your church to watch? Taking advantage of the video technology to reach the younger generation is a huge step forward for the iChurch.

What does all this cost? Without considering the cost to actually record the sermon or event, the cost is free or minimal. Once you have shot the video, it can be uploaded to YouTube, Vimeo and Facebook for free. The downside with YouTube.com, Facebook and Vimeo is the twenty-minute time limit on videos. Vimeo.com provides the solution to this limit with its pro version which allows for unlimited length on videos. The Pro version costs money. But Vimeo.com is worth it and heavily used by the iChurch. If your church is small and just getting started, with one digital video recorder, some free software and a twenty-minute limit to YouTube.com, your church can become a large iChurch. Technology is a wonderful thing!

Audio

Audio delivery methods are fairly simple. Apple's mobile device iPod and its iTunes software do the heavy lifting in audio downloads. iTunes makes it easy to download audio straight to a user's computer or iPod. Many users have already downloaded the free iTunes software so downloading a digital file to their device is easy and quick. The format of the audio file is usually a MP3 file.

If your church has the ability to record audio separately, you can create the same products as video. Live streaming audio is used like a radio station of the old days. Archiving the audio can be done the same way as video. Taking a little time to label the audio files with keywords can turn them into a wonderful library for online users. Your iChurch should really pay attention to audio because more and more website visitors are downloading the audio files as podcasts to their iPods. When you see people jogging or working out with headphones on, you might assume they are listening to their favorite music. That is not always the case. Statistics bear this out. These folks working out or simply driving to and from work may be listening to a podcast that teaches them a new language, reads a book to them or plays last week's sermon from your church. Do not underestimate the power of your church's audio recordings.

The great news for audio recordings is the cost. Most everything is free. The reason is the files themselves are smaller than video and much easier to transfer through an internet connection. They are also easy to cut up into multiple products (repurposing).

What are some of the audio product ideas for the iChurch?
- Bible passage readings;
- Weekly sermons;
- Portions of books produced by the pastor of the church;
- Guest speakers;
- Church meetings;
- A list of current church activities; and
- Telephone interviews of missionaries.

Obviously, there are many more examples but this should get you started. Don't overlook the power of audio in your iChurch.

Images

Since we addressed images, their benefits and how they should be optimized and used on the website, we won't go into that again. But the one thing we will talk about here is where to find good images for your ministry website in case you don't have any of your church in action. The best website to find images is www.istockphoto.com. They have a great selection of royalty-free photos that can be used on your church's website. Type in "church service" in the search bar and see the photos you can purchase for around $10.

Documents

We have talked about using video and audio but what about combining technology with plain old written words? Creating products in document form is very easy and mostly free. Let's start with a simple document you might generate in Microsoft Word. Assume your church is generating a list of all the missionaries it supports along with their contact information, area of the world they are working in and a short background of the missionary. You church wants to puts this on the website for members and website visitors to pray for, support and know what the church is doing on the missionary front. Once you create this document in Word, you simply save it as a PDF (Portable Document Format). This feature is in current versions of Word and also available online for free by typing into Google the search "how to turn documents into pdf" and looking through the free programs. Once you have the PDF, your programmer simply uploads it to your site as a link that can be clicked on by any online user. The PDF document can also be downloaded to the user's site and printed out. Creating PDF's and uploading them to your site allows for quick dissemination of information from the church leadership to its members.

Another way to upload a document to your website is to actually upload it to someone else's site and place a link to the document on your website. Websites like Docstoc.com, scribd.com, docs.google.com and issuu.com are some great examples. When you subscribe to one of these sites (usually for free), you can upload documents and receive a link that can be placed on your website. You can always upload documents in their native format such as .docx, xlsx, pdf, and pptx, which when clicked will require that the online user have Microsoft Office installed on their computer or smart phone. Another way to make these files more easily viewable by all website visitors is to upload them to an online provider such as scribd.com and they are converted into a web format that is viewable on computer, mobile devices and smart phones.

With additional minimal effort, a church newsletter can be generated and sent automatically by email to members or any subscriber. We call these *eNewsletters*. An eNewsletter can be simple or you can purchase software to make better versions with advanced graphics and images.

Digital magazines are similar to eNewsletters but focus on a particular subject matter rather than church events. Digital magazines are usually produced in PDF form

Has the pastor or someone in the church written a book? An *eBook* is now easy and fast. With the book written and in Word or PDF, there are sites that allow this content to be quickly uploaded and translated into the publishing company's format. Once this happens, you or someone working for you, can layout the text to look more appropriate. A cover can be designed usually for free and added to the front. If the book is given away for free, there are less additional costs. If the book is going to be sold, there are a few other costs such as registering it with the copyright office (usually $35) and purchasing a ISBN ($100 to $200) which is a number that allows for the book to be sold. eBooks are exploding in popularity with Amazon recently claiming it sells more eBooks than printed books.

eBooks have some big advantages. Once you have written the book, the process can take less than a week to upload and begin selling it. Also, when someone downloads your book, it is very difficult for someone else to read it for free. This means that the writer (you) can collect a fee for everyone who reads it. And it's much cheaper to transmit an eBook to a reader's computer, smart phone or Kindle than to print up a thousand copies, ship them by truck, store them, sort them, label them, prevent shoplifting and worry about what happens to all these copies if they don't sell. The content for an eBook takes more time to generate, but eBooks can certainly generate additional income as well as expand the message of the iChurch.

iChurch Media Center

Imagine that your church has fully embraced multimedia and is busy generating video, audio and document products for the iChurch when someone asks, "Where on the website do all these items go?" Good question. The answer is the iChurch Media Center. Let's look at an example.

T.D. Jakes Ministries and The Potter's House have a great example of an iChurch Media Center. To get there you go to http://www.thepottershouse.org/Multimedia/Internet-Church.aspx. (See the image on the next page)

When online users arrive, they are greeted with several options. On the far right are four tabs to choose from. The first tab displayed is *Events*. Notice a vertical list of products with the first choice asking the user to become a subscriber. The next tab *Bible* provides an online bible that is supplied by Youversion.com. This is a terrific resource for numerous versions of the bible. The next tab is Facebook. This is the *Fan Page* tab of the ministry's Facebook page. Here, you can see the Facebook updates and "Like" the page by joining it via Facebook. The last tab is *Salvation*. Located on this tab are video and audio messages from Bishop T.D. Jakes about salvation and how to obtain it.

Occasionally, additional tabs are added such as Twitter, Donate and Chat, but right now those tabs are disabled.

Go to the left side of this Multimedia page and you will find a choice between two online broadcasts: *Dallas* and *North Dallas*. These two buttons give the user the option to watch the live service from The Potter's House of Dallas with Bishop T.D. Jakes or The Potter's House of North Dallas with Pastor Sheryl Brady. Right below those two buttons is a button called *Donate* along with two drop-down menus. Look how simple it is to donate money! The user simply types in an amount, chooses the category and clicks donate. Then, the user is walked through a few steps to collect the money from their credit card. Beneath the Donate button is the video module where an online user actually sees the broadcast. There are options below it such as Windows, Flash 1 and Flash 2. These options let the user choose multiple viewing streams depending on their preference, online connection and computer. Beneath all that we see the Potter's House logo, broadcast times and message letting users know that the Sunday message is rebroadcast all day for their viewing pleasure. Finally, we see social media integration with the Facebook Like button and the number of people that have "liked" this webpage. The *Share* icon allows the user to tell people that the user is on this webpage and that they should join the user.

You should go to this website and explore the ways they have taken full advantage of multimedia to extend the iChurch. The best part about the iChurch Media Center is that it's only limited by what you think should go there. You can add an option to view archived weekly sermons and let the user choose which message to watch. You can add a chat tab so that people can communicate while watching your videos, you can add a notes feature where people can take notes while watching your videos or live message and email it to themselves or friends. The options are unlimited. There are many companies that create iChurch media centers. One, of course, is the company that created this book, which is Caston Digital (www.theichurchmethod.com). Other good ones are Lifechurch's Church Online (http://churchonline.org/), Streaming Faith's Online Campus (http://sales.streamingfaith.com/online-campus), and StreamingChurch.TV (http://streamingchurch.tv/).

Overall, multimedia should play a major role in the implementation of your iChurch strategy. There should be videos on your homepage, live streaming Sunday services, audio/video podcasts of sermons, inspirational messages available via iTunes, and video archives of past sermons online for people to watch. For more information on how to implement these strategies, read "Tech Talk" below.

What I Want For My iChurch - Part 2

(a) I want multimedia on my website.

(b) I want the following video for my website:

    1. On-Demand Video.

    2. Live Streaming Video.

    3. Podcasts.

(c) Here are the specific video items I want on my website:

    1. Live weekly sermons.

    2. Archived sermons.

    3. Searchable directory.

    4. Videos of ministry work.

    5. Videos of community activities.

    6. Videos of guest speakers.

(d) Add access points to my website from:

    1. Facebook.

    2. Twitter.

    3. Google Plus.

(e) Upload my videos to:

    1. YouTube.

    2. Vimeo.

    3. FaceBook.

4. Vimeo Pro version (I will pay the cost because I want videos to be longer than 20 minutes).

5. My own server.

(f) I want the following audio items for my website:

1. Live podcasts of weekly sermons.

2. Archived podcasts of past sermons.

3. Bible passage readings.

4. Searchable directory.

5. Portions of books produced by the pastor of the church.

6. Guest speakers.

7. Church meetings.

8. A list of current church activities

9. Telephone interviews of missionaries.

(g) I want high quality images for my website.

(h) I want the following documents on my website:

1. eNewsletters.

2. Digital magazines.

3. eBooks.

(i) I want documents on my website uploaded to:

1. Docstoc.com.

2. scribd.com.

3. docs.google.com.

4. issuu.com.

5. My own server.

(j) I want the following tabs on my website:

1. Events

2. Bible

3. Facebook

4. Salvation

5. Donate

6. Locations

(k) I want to hire this company to help build my iChurch:

1. Caston Digital (http://www.theichurchmethod.com)
2. Lifechurch's Church Online (http://churchonline.org/).
3. Streaming Faith's Online Campus (http://sales.streamingfaith.com/online-campus).
4. StreamingChurch.tv (http://streamingchurch.tv/)

Let's Talk Tech

How to create multiple products from a sermon

A question that I am often asked is: "How can a preacher put his sermon online?" This question is usually the gateway question to the real question that preachers want to know which is "How can I *sell* my sermons online?" I simply respond, "If you would like to, I can help you turn one sermon into four products."

In order to turn a sermon into four separate revenue-generating products, a church must have a few items. These include a computer (preferably a Mac), iTunes media software, Video Camera with microphone, ImTOO Video Convertor Standard Video conversion software (imtoo.com), Google Docs Account (or Adobe Acrobat Full version and Microsoft Word) and a PayPal Business account.

Step 1. Preach Sermon

The first step in this entire process is to create the content. Normally, for most churches it's the pastor's sermon. The pastor's sermon is the actual message preached during service as well as the notes, if any, that accompany the sermon. The first task is to video record the sermon. Make sure the video recording is done with a good quality camera and has a microphone attachment to capture good quality audio. I would suggest a flip camera (http://www.theflip.com/) with a wireless lapel microphone. Some churches like to put a lapel microphone on the pastor that wirelessly (Bluetooth or another method) connects with the camera so that the audio is automatically transferred to the video recording. You can also get a high quality microphone attachment to put on the camera to make sure the camera can accurately hear the pastor during his sermon.

Keep sermon notes for book conversion by typing them up in Microsoft Word or Google Docs.

Step 2. Convert Sermon to CD and mp3

The first two products will be a CD and an mp3 file to sell. To begin, take the recorded video file of the live sermon and put it into the ImTOO software. Convert the video file into an mp3 file. You can sell this mp3 file in your online store as a digital download and sell it for $1.99 - $3.99.

Next, you can create a CD to sell. Take the mp3 that was created and import it to iTunes on a mac or PC. From iTunes, burn the mp3 to a CD, put the CD in a clear plastic case and sell the CD in the online store and/or church bookstore.

Step 3. Convert Sermon to DVD and mp4

The final two products to create are a DVD and an mp4 file. Let's start with the mp4. The high quality video recording of the pastor's sermon should be in mp4 format from your video camera. If it is not, take the video file that was recorded and put it into the ImTOO software. Then, convert the video file into a mp4 file (example specs are video size 640 x 480, bitrate 1200kbps, max bitrate 2500kbps, audio bitrate 64kbps, sample rate 48000hz, every other setting can be left as the default). This mp4 file is a more universal format for videos because it works on Macs and PCs (as does Windows Media but mp4 is better). Take this mp4 file and put it on the online store as a download and sell it for $3.99 - $6.99.

Next, we need to create a DVD to sell. Take the mp4 that was created and download ImTOO DVD creator or Nero Suite and use that software to turn the video file into a DVD. Sell that DVD in the online store and/or church bookstore.

If you want, take the mp4 file and put it on youtube.com and vimeo.com so that people can watch your messages for free and generate a buzz. Inside the description of the videos put a link to purchase the message in your online store. You don't have to put all your messages on youtube.com and vimeo.com but putting a few up there would be a great marketing tool to help people get familiar with your ministry.

Once you have these items setup then the process of adding products to your online store and distributing your future mp3s and mp4s will be significantly easier.

Next, let's look at how to add multimedia to your ministry website. Well, the process to add documents to your site in flash (and HTML5) format is done via a website called scribd.com. Scribd.com was created so that "anyone can instantly upload and transform any file -- including PDF, Word and PowerPoint -- into a web document that's discoverable through search engines, shared on social networks and read on billions of mobile devices" (Scribd.com, 2010).

Upload PDF, Word, Excel and Powerpoint documents to scribd
Step 1. Login to the scribd website at scribd.com by clicking "Log in" or "Sign Up" in the top right corner. You can also use the "Login with Facebook" option if you have a Facebook account.

Once you click on one of the options at the top right you will see the screen on the next page.

Step 2. After you have logged in (or signed up for a new account and then logged in) you can now upload a document into scribd. This document can be either a PDF, Word, Excel, or PPT document. Click on the large blue "Upload" button at the top left near the Scribd logo.

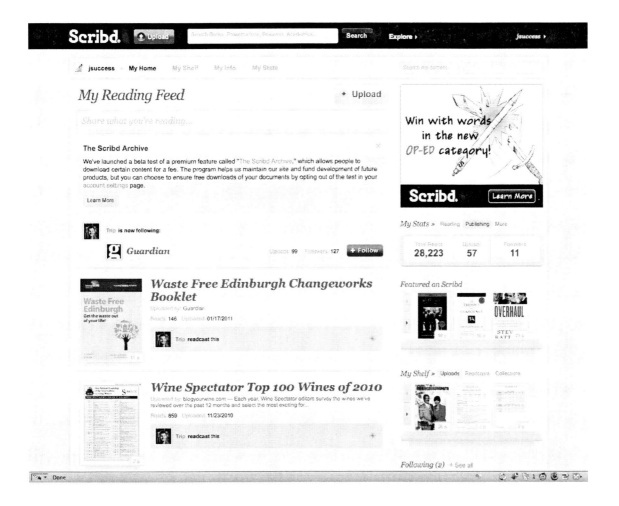

Step 3. Once you click the blue "Upload" button, you will get the page below where you can either:

1. Select a file to upload;

2. Import your Google docs from your Google account;

3. Sell your documents in the scribd store;

4. Enter text and create a scribd document right on the fly.

For our focus we will use option 1 and select a file to upload. Therefore, click the blue "Upload" button and choose the document you want to upload from your computer.

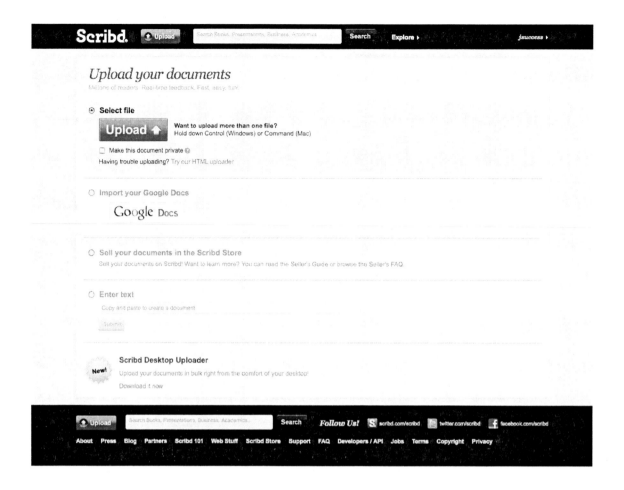

Step 4. Once the file has completed uploading, you will get the page below where you fill out information about the file you just uploaded. You can choose whatever category you want the document to go in, add tags so that the document can be categorized accordingly and you can add a description. Finally, hit save and the document is saved in your scribd document files.

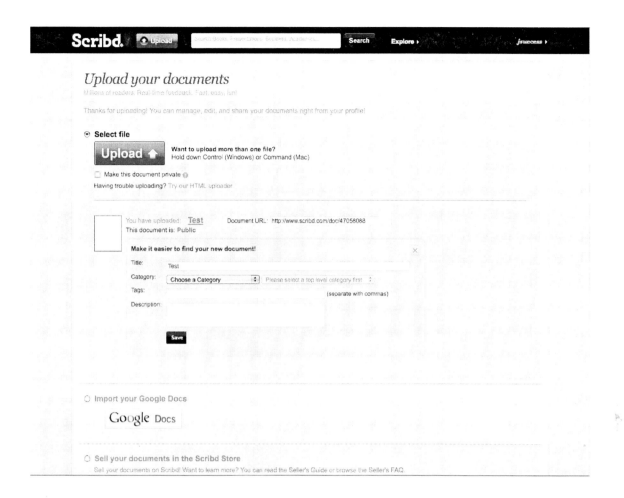

If you ever need to update the document or change any information on it, you can click on the document's name and you will get the page below. From here you can choose to "Upload a Revision" to update the document or you can "Edit/Delete" the document and change the description information that you added previously. Also, remember to make your documents public so that people can see your documents from anywhere.

If you decide to "Edit/Delete" your document then you will get the screen on the next page.

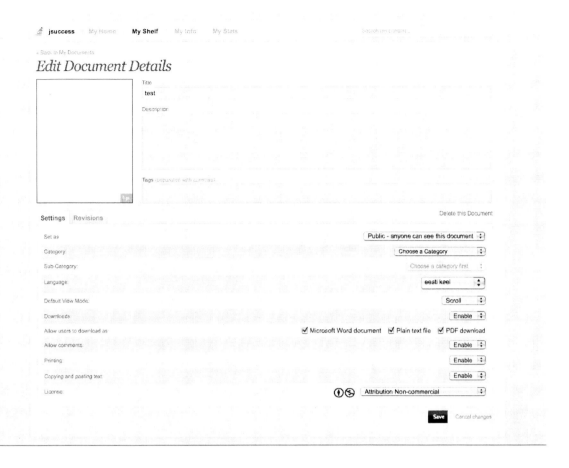

If you decide to select the "Upload a Revision" option then you will get the page below. You will then need to go to the bottom of the page and click the link that says "Publish a new version of this document." You will then choose the updated version of the document from your computer and it will update the document in scribd as well as on any pages that you have embedded this scribd document on.

Step 5. Finally, now that we have uploaded our document, we need to get the code so that we can embed it in webpages on our website. To do this you click on the document's name to get back to the page where you were before and you could select "Edit/Delete" and "Upload a Revision." Beneath those options, a bit down the page is an option that says "Share and Embed." Here you can choose where you want to share your file at, Facebook, Twitter, Buzz or Embed. You want to choose the "Embed" option because this will give you the screen below and you can get the "standard HTML" code that you can put onto a webpage and the document you uploaded will be viewable from any browser.

Create a Podcast with Podbean

Many churches would like to know the easiest way to get their sermons, videos and messages onto iTunes as podcasts. Here is one of the ways to do it. This process uses a popular service called Podbean (podbean.com) and is very affordable. Keep in mind that this process is based on the assumption that you have your podcasts files (audio or video) already completed and ready to be sent out to the world. If you have not created a video or audio file then please do that first.

Step 1. Go to Podbean.com and click on "Sign up" in the upper right hand corner

Step 2. Click on "Sign Up Now" in the "Basic" column to create your free account

Step 3. Fill out all the information that the page is asking for and then at the bottom of the page click "Order now." Make sure you write down your username and password.

PodBean.COM Podcast hosting, Social subscribing

Search

Home | Podcasts | Tags | Add a Podcast | Publish a podcast | Advertising

▶ PodBean Professional

Create Your Account

⊡ Member Name : _____ . **podbean.com**

You cannot change this name so choose carefully.
You can set own domain(ex.podcast.yourdomain.com) at a later time.

Personal information

⊡ Email : _____

⊡ First Name : _____

⊡ Last Name : _____

⊡ Password : _____   Please input 6 - 12 characters

⊡ Confirm
Password : _____

⊡ Country : _____

⊡ Postal code : _____

⊡ Gender :   ○ Female   ○ Male

⊡ Date of Birth :   Month ↕ / Day ↕ / Year ↕
You must be at least 13 years of age.

⊡ Service
Agreement :   ☐ By checking the box you agree to the Podbean.com Terms of Service

⊡ Payment
Option: [Podbean Professional – $99.5/yr ↕]

Save 17%! Just $8.29/month!
30 Days Money Back Guarantee for Annual Plan

⊡ Coupon code
(optional) : _____   (Apply)

☑ Yes, email me Podbean newsletter.

[Order Now]

Step 4. Retrieve your Login Name and Password from the email sent to you from Podbean. Go to podbean.com and enter your username and password from the email and click "Login."

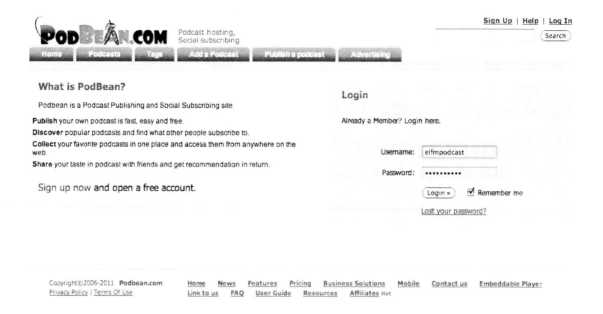

Step 5. Click on "Skip for Now" if asked to upload a photo. You may want to change your password to something else so it will be easy to remember. Next, in the right column at the bottom, click on "My Dashboard" to get to the section to publish your first show.

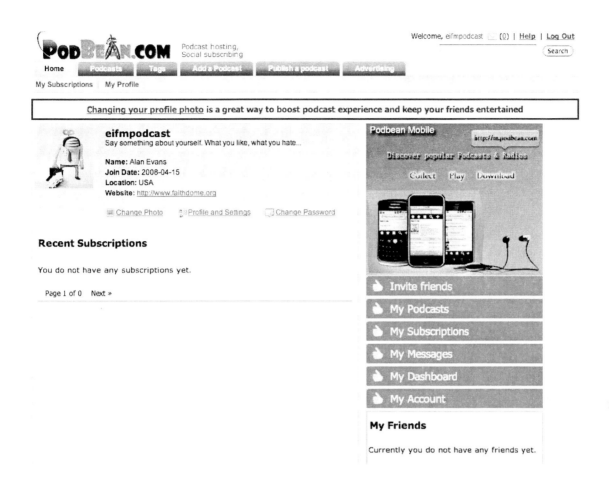

Step 6. This is the dashboard page. This is the page that we use to get to a variety of options such as adjusting our iTunes settings under the "Settings" tab or creating a new podcast by clicking on the "Publish a new show" option. First, let's fill in the settings of our podcast so that it displays correctly. At the right there is a "Settings" tab/link. Please click on that.

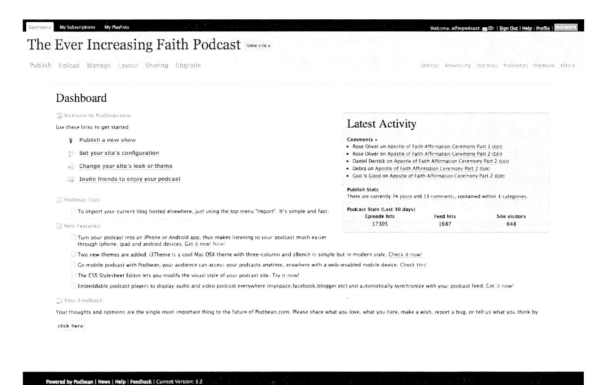

First we want to fill in the "General Options" information.

- **Channel Privacy** - we want to choose **Public.**

- **Channel Logo** – upload a logo for your podcast, this can be a church logo or a photo of the pastor.

- **Channel Title** – Pick a title for your Podcast (ex. ABC Church Podcasts).

- **Chanel Category** – Choose Religion.

- **Channel tags** – choose 3 – 5 keywords that describe your ministry.

- **Brief Description** – give a brief description of the podcast and your ministry.

- **E-mail address** – give a general email address of the ministry that someone can respond to about the podcasts.

- **Copyright** – Input the copyright statement for the church's podcasts. A good example is **Copyright 2011** – ABC Church. All Rights Reserved.

- **Editor Selection** – check this box.

- **Navigation Bar** – check this box.

- **Click the "Update Options" button.**

Next we want to click on the Feed/iTunes option that is next to the General tab. This is where we configure our podcast for iTunes. At the top of the page is an iTunes preview that you can use to see what your podcast will look like in iTunes. Fill in the following fields.

- First you want to copy the "Your RSS Feed" link because that is what you will input into iTunes.

- **iTunes FeedID:** Leave this blank for now, we will come back to this

- **iTunes Summary:** Use the summary from before that you used to describe your podcast

- **iTunes: Podcast logo:** Upload a custom Podcast logo or use the logo that you uploaded before.

- **iTunes Author/owner:** Input the name of the Author or owner of the podcasts. This is usually the pastor's name.

- **iTunes Subtitle:** Choose a subtitle for your podcasts.

- **iTunes Categories:** Choose categories that describe your ministry and podcast. I would suggest Religion & Spirituality: Christianity, and other religious categories.

- **iTunes Email:** Input an email address of someone that can respond on behalf of the ministry to podcast or inquiries.

- **iTunes Explicit:** Choose Clean.

- **iTunes TTL** : 1.

- **iTunes Block:** No.

- **Language:** English.

- **Show Download Links in RSS Encoded Content:** No.

- **Link URL in RSS2:** Leave blank.

- **Additional Feed Entity:** Leave blank.

- Finally, open up iTunes and make sure you have that copy of the "Your RSS Feed" link because that is what you will input into iTunes.

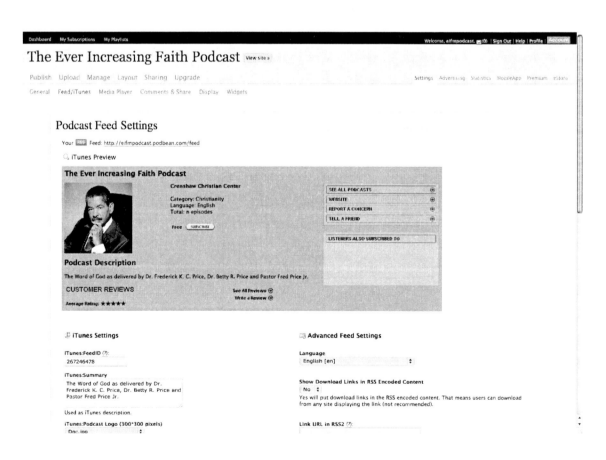

Now that you have iTunes open, make sure you are on the iTunes store homepage. At the bottom of the page in the footer in the first column there is a "Podcasts" option. Click that.

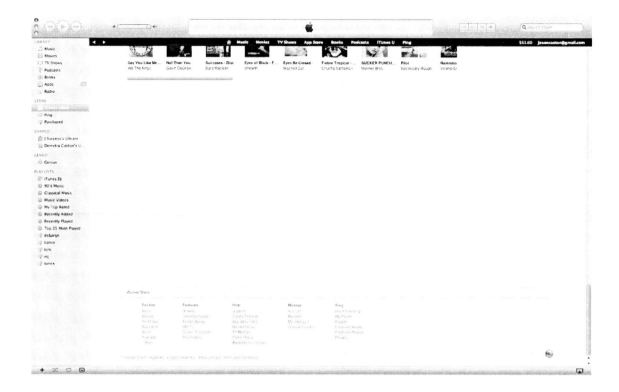

On the right side you will see an option to submit podcasts, click on that.

80

Finally, you will see a page where you submit the "Your RSS Feed" link that you copied earlier. Once you submit this, you will receive an email at the iTunes account that you are using and it will acknowledge that apple has received a Podcast submission. Within 24 hours you should receive another email that says the Podcast has been added (or rejected with reason why, and then you can go in and make changes and resubmit the RSS Feed). Once your podcast is accepted, you can then find the iTunes FeedID that we skipped before and input the number that iTunes gave you that is associated with your podcast.

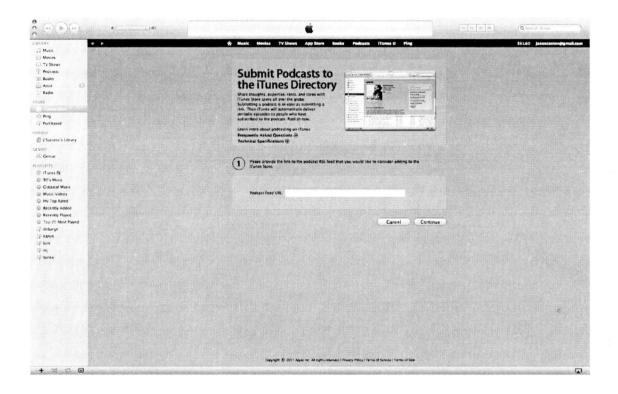

Step 7. Now go back to podbean and click on the Publish tab on the left. This will get you to the actual Podcast page. Here is where you can create a podcast. First, you have to fill in the tags with keywords that describe your podcasts. Next, you want to give your show a professional and accurate title. Next, type a brief description of your podcast. When you get down to the section "Add Media File" you want to click on "Choose File" and upload your video/audio file from your computer. Scroll down and click "Publish!" Once uploaded, click "View site" and you will be able to see your podcast on

podbean.com. You can also go over to iTunes and see your podcast there. Just open up iTunes and do a search for the title of your podcast. It normally takes 24 hours for iTunes to get the podcast initially loaded up but once they have the initial process setup, you should see your podcasts on iTunes within 30 minutes of publishing them in podbean.

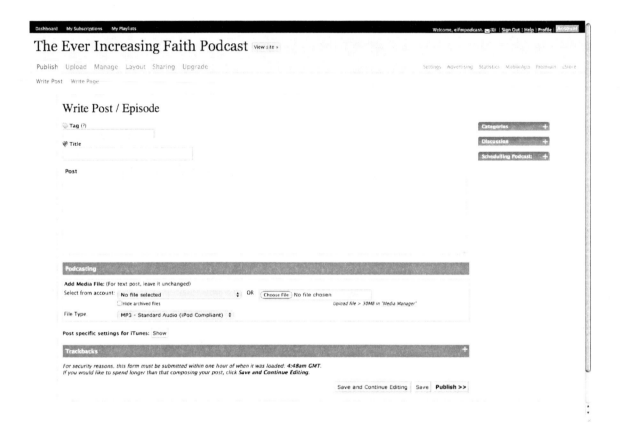

How to stream a sermon live

First, we will address how to stream a live sermon and then we will speak on how to stream an on-demand, prerecorded sermon.

Live Sermons:

You need to make sure you have these things:

- Computer (preferably a laptop).
- Ustream.tv account.
- Camera (webcam or camcorder).
- (optional) Microphone that can connect to the camera or the computer.

Now that you have these items, let's get started.

1. Set up your camera on your computer. Make sure that your computer can recognize your camera and your microphone. These items come with installation instructions based on the type of camera so I won't go into depth with that.

2. Set up a ustream.tv account if you already haven't done so. Go to ustream.tv and click on "Login" if you already have an account. Or click on "Sign Up" if you do not have an account.

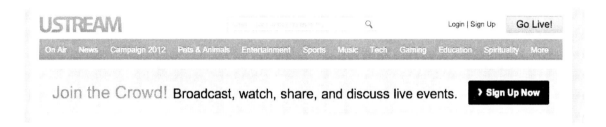

Once you have your account set up, you need to create a channel. This will be what your ustream channel will be called. Click the "Create a New Channel" Link on the left.

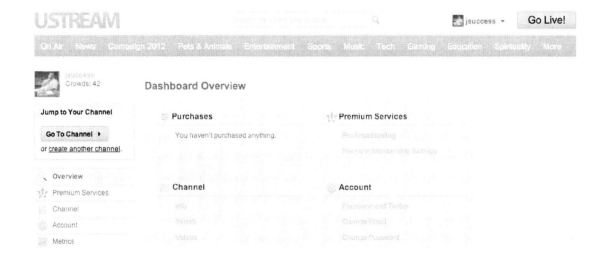

I named my channel **theonebibleshow** and therefore my ustream channel was located at http://www.ustream.tv/channel/**theonebibleshow.** This is the link that you can give to your viewers or put on your website so that people can view your show at the ustream website. Later, we will go into how to stream your show directly on your website.

Your Channel's name   ✖

Type in the name of your channel and click Create.

theonebibleshow

Create or cancel

You will then be asked a few questions about your show and after that you are ready to start broadcasting live.

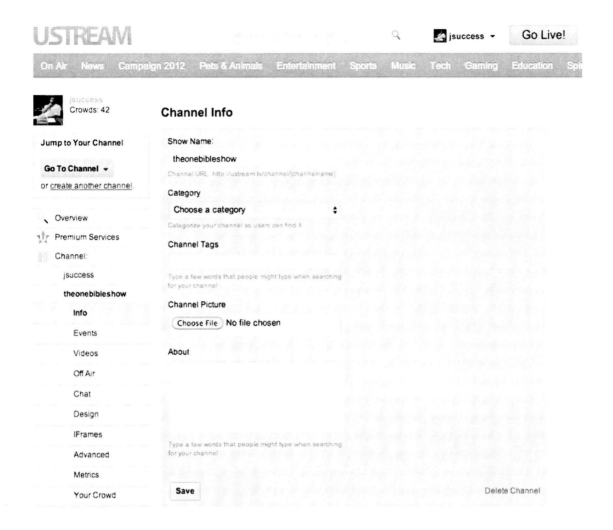

After completing all the information above "click Save" at the bottom of the page. Next, you need to test your camera to make sure you can see your designated target, whether it is the pulpit, a stage or a sermon from your desk. To test your camera (and your microphone), once you login click the "Go Live" button, located at the top right area of the page. After that you will be prompted to connect to your camera. Once that is complete, you will see a live video stream coming from your camera. It should look similar to the screen on the next page.

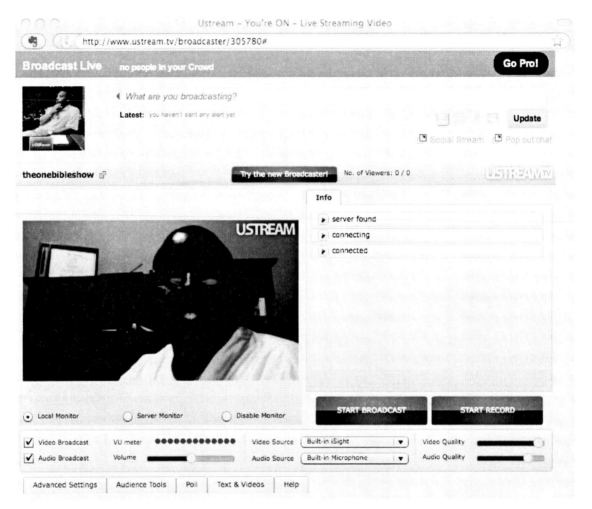

Now that you are done testing, you are ready to broadcast your message to the world. Click on "Start Broadcast" and "Start Record." That's it! Once you are done broadcasting, click on "Stop Broadcast" and "Stop Record." You will then see a "Recordings" tab right next to the "Info" asking if you want to save the recording. Make sure you select "yes" because that recording can be shown over and over.

3. Finally, now that we have the show complete, we can go to our ustream page and get the embed codes. This is where you will need someone with some technical expertise because the embed code is what you want to copy and paste onto your website page. You can copy this code and paste it prior to starting your broadcast so that people can come directly to your site to see your online message instead of coming to ustream.tv.

If you would like some information from ustream.tv on what camera devices the service is compatible with, please go to http://helpcenter.ustream.tv/content/recommended-cameras-and-equipment.

How to Show Archived Sermons

Archived sermons are slightly different than live sermons in that you record the sermon first and then make it viewable on your website or social networking site at a later time. This process is very similar to the live format but has a few different steps.

1. Record sermon (if you record it on ustream then leave it on there).
2. Upload to vimeo, YouTube or ustream.
3. Get link from vimeo, YouTube or ustream.
4. Put link on website.

First, let's look at the things we will need.
1. A camcorder (preferably in HD), and preferably with a microphone. It would be much easier if you get one that can mount on a tripod to remain steady.
2. A computer that you can connect with your camcorder after you are finished recording your sermon and upload your digital video file.
3. An account on YouTube (if your sermon is under 20 minutes then you can put it on YouTube for free), vimeo (if your sermon is over 20 minutes then get a vimeo professional account that costs $60 per year).

Now that you have these items, let's get started.
1. Step one. Record your sermon onto your camcorder. Then connect the camcorder to your computer to upload the digital file to your computer's desktop.
2. Step two. It's time to upload the video to the Internet. For demonstration purposes, I will show you how to upload to youtube.com first, then show you how to upload to vimeo.com.

After you have saved your sermon to your computer's desktop, go to youtube.com and "**Sign In**" (or Create Account if you don't have one already) to your account at the top right of the page.

Once you are signed in, click "**Upload**" at the top of the page.

You then will see the actual "**Upload Video**" page, where you click the "**Upload Video**" yellow button in the middle of the page.

After you click the "**Upload Video**" a window will popup that will let you choose the file you want to upload from your desktop. Once you choose the file, the upload process will begin and you will be able to watch the progress, fill in the video information and set the privacy settings.

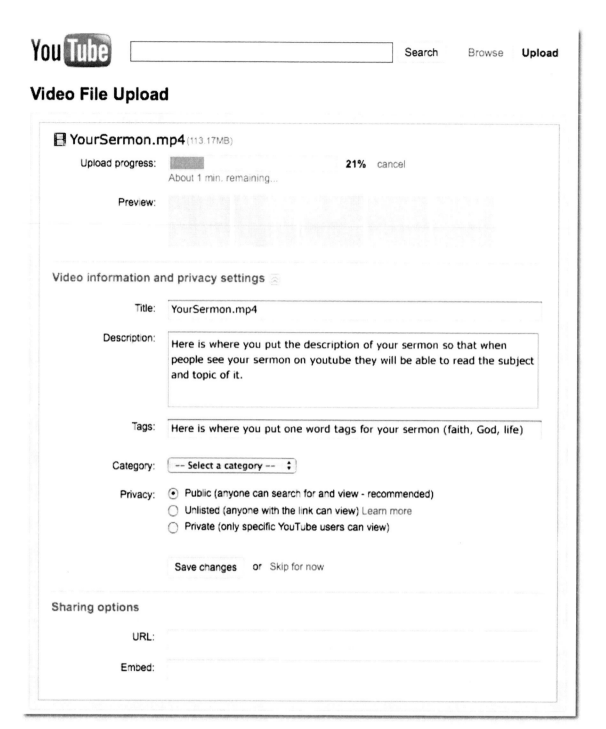

Once you have completed that information, you just have to wait for the file to be uploaded before you can receive the YouTube URL (webpage) and the Embed code that you can use to put the video on your own website.

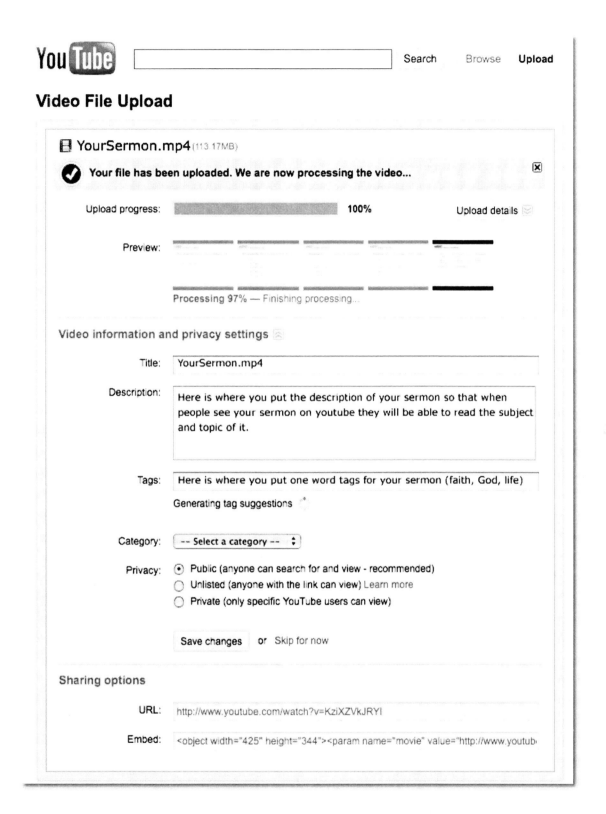

Now that you have the Embed code, this is where you will need someone with some technical expertise because the embed code is what you want to copy and paste onto your website page. You can copy this code and paste it prior to starting your broadcast so that people can come directly to your site to see your online message and not have to come to youtube.com.

If your video is over 20 minutes, then you will need to use a paid service such as vimeo.com. Here are the steps to upload a video to vimeo.com.

After you have saved your sermon to your computer's desktop, go to vimeo.com and "**Log In**" (or "**Join Vimeo**" if you don't already have an account) to your account at the top right of the page with your email address and password.

Once you are signed in, you then click on "**Upload**" at the top of the page.

You will then see the actual "**Upload Video**" page, where you click on the "**Choose a**

file to upload" blue button in the middle of the page.

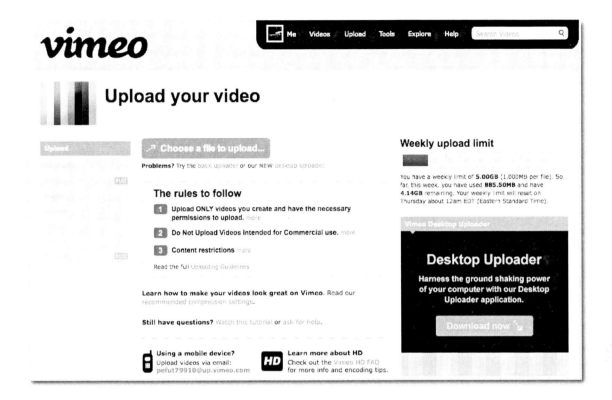

After you click the "**Choose a file to upload...**" blue button, a window will popup that will let you choose the file you want to upload from your desktop. Once you choose the file, the upload process will begin and you will be able to watch the upload progress, fill in the video basic information, privacy information, credits information, license information, add to information, photos information and embedding information. But we will wait until the video is processed to fill all that out.

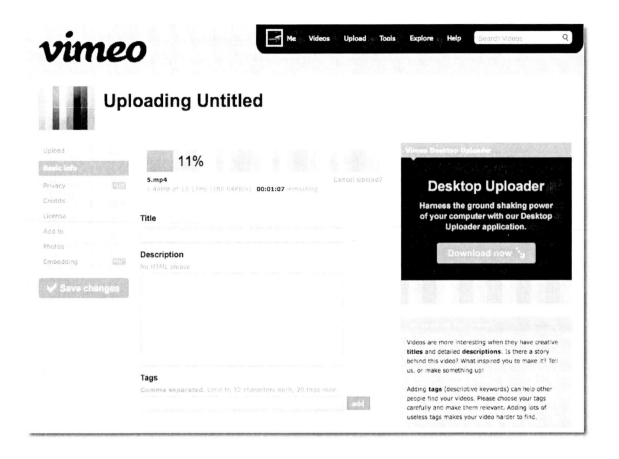

Once the video is uploaded and done processing, we can go in and fill out the additional video information, which is under the "Settings" tab for the video. Let's first fill in the basic information, which is the Title of the Video, the description and the one-word tags.

After you have completed all of that, you can then click the "Privacy" tab beneath it. Here you can determine who can see your video and who cannot. You can choose if you want people to see your video on vimeo.com. You can choose which particular people you want to see your video. Here are the easiest answers for these questions:

- Who can see this video? **Hide this video from Vimeo.com.**
- Where can this video appear? **Anywhere.**
- What can people do with this video? **Don't check any of these options.**
- Who can post comments on this video? **Only my contacts.**

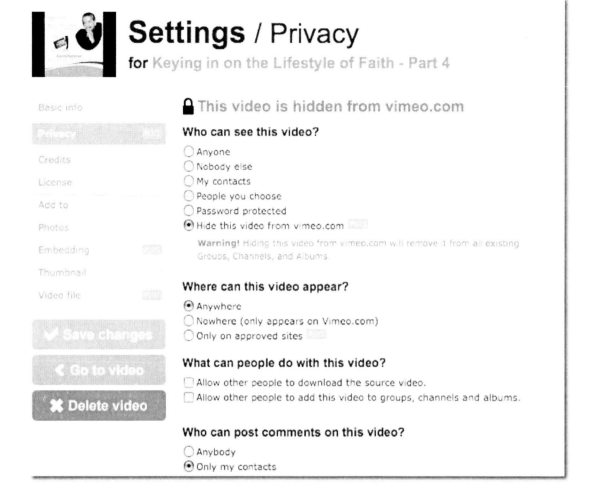

After you have completed that, let's jump down to the "Embedding" tab below it. Here you are determining what type of "controls" (play button, logo, share button) appear on your video when you embed it in your website. For now, let's leave Intro as it is, leave Outro as it is and under Everything else, ONLY CHECK:

- Show playbar.
- Volume Control.
- Fullscreen Button.
- Scaling button.

and that's it.

Settings / Embedding

for Keying in on the Lifestyle of Faith - Part 4

Basic info

Privacy PLUS

Credits

License

Add to

Photos

Embedding PLUS

Thumbnail

Video file PLUS

✔ Save changes

‹ Go to video

✖ Delete video

Preview your embedded video

Get embed code

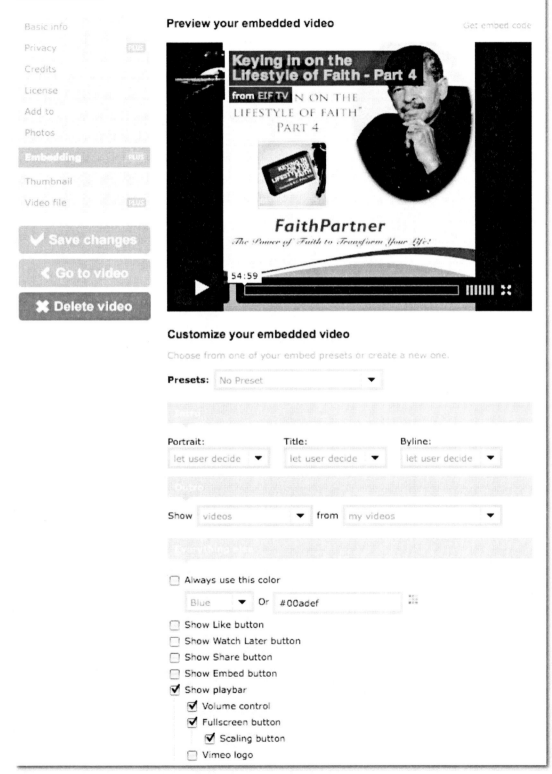

Customize your embedded video

Choose from one of your embed presets or create a new one.

Presets: No Preset ▼

Portrait:	Title:	Byline:
let user decide ▼	let user decide ▼	let user decide ▼

Show videos ▼ from my videos ▼

☐ Always use this color

Blue ▼ Or #00adef

☐ Show Like button
☐ Show Watch Later button
☐ Show Share button
☐ Show Embed button
☑ Show playbar
   ☑ Volume control
   ☑ Fullscreen button
      ☑ Scaling button
   ☐ Vimeo logo

After you have completed that, let's jump down to the "Thumbnail" tab below it. Here you choose the thumbnail or image that you want to appear when people get to your video. Prior to the video starting, there is an image that is shown with your video and this image is called the thumbnail. In vimeo, you get to choose that thumbnail based on preset screenshots taken from your video. Otherwise, if you want to upload your own image of a logo or a set picture for your video, then you can click "**Choose a file to upload**" under "**Upload your own thumbnail**" and select a picture from your computer.

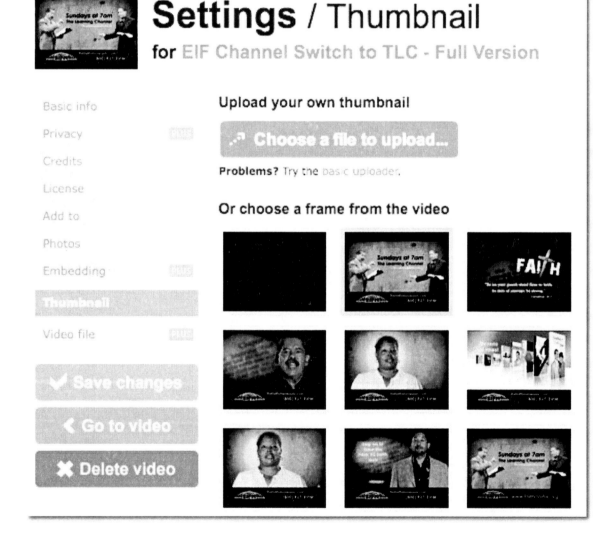

Now that you have completed all these steps, click on the blue "Save changes" button and then click on the green "Go to video" button to see your video page. Once you are at your video page, you can get the Embed code you will need for your own website. To get the video code, you click on the "embed" button that is on the actual video.

After you have clicked that button, you will see a popup with the embed code for your video. There are two versions of the embed code. One version is the new version which is an <iframe> version for iPads, iPhones and sites that will be seen on mobile devices.

Embed this video

NEW! This is our new embed code which supports iPad, iPhone, Flash and beyond. Don't like change? Use the old embed code instead.

Get the embed code

```
<iframe src="http://player.vimeo.com/video/15783271?byline=0&amp;portrait=0" width="400" height="295" frameborder="0"></iframe>
```

Preview the embedded video

FaithPartner Digital Product

The other embed code is the "old" embed code and it's used on the majority of websites. This code looks similar to what you would have received from youtube.com or ustream.com.

Embed this video

NEW! Try our new embed code which supports iPad, iPhone, Flash and beyond.

Get the embed code

```
<object width="400" height="295"><param name="allowfullscreen"
value="true" /><param name="allowscriptaccess" value="always"
/><param name="movie" value="http://vimeo.com
/moogaloop.swf?clip_id=15783271&amp;server=vimeo.com&
amp;show_title=1&amp;show_byline=0&amp;show_portrait=0&
```

Preview the embedded video

FaithPartner Digital Product

Now that you have the Embed code, you will need someone with some technical expertise because the embed code is what you want to copy and paste onto your website page. You can copy this code and paste it prior to starting your broadcast so that people can come directly to your site to see your online message and not have to come to vimeo.com.

Part 3
Ecommerce: Online Stores/Online Donations

Let's Talk Strategy

What is eCommerce?

The word eCommerce is everywhere. But what does it actually mean? Simple. eCommerce is short for Electronic Commerce. The word "commerce" generally refers to the trading of goods and services, the moving of products from one place to another with money exchanged in the process. So, add the word "electronic" to commerce and you have the ability to conduct financial transactions over the internet.

I am sure you have already experienced eCommerce in one way or another. Have you ever used Apple iTunes, eBay or Amazon.com? Amazon is the largest eCommerce site/business in the world. More than anyone else, they sell products like books, DVDs, electronics, mp3s, eBooks and a variety of other goods. The most amazing aspect of this is that they receive money for it without ever physically touching or seeing the customer. Their business model is *the* business model for eCommerce.

Mimicking Amazon's online buying experience is always a great strategy. You can easily and safely purchase something from Amazon and see it at your doorstep a few days later or download it immediately. Likewise, Apple iTunes is the largest digital media store in the world. They sell songs, movies, TV shows, eBooks and a variety of other digital downloads. Apple iTunes and Amazon sells digital downloads that you can pay for securely, download seamlessly and listen to easily. This simple process is what makes their eCommerce stores so successful.

By the way, eCommerce is projected to reach $197 billion by the end of 2011. It is interesting to note that when the recession hit, buying through eCommerce continued to increase at an accelerating pace. The bottomline is that if you are not using eCommerce for the iChurch, you are losing out big time!

How can eCommerce enhance The iChurch Method?

There are several ways eCommerce can help the iChurch. Here are the main features you need to consider when thinking about your own website and eCommerce.

Online Donations - The effectiveness of online donations cannot be denied. Online donations hit their stride in 2008 during the political campaign of Barack Obama. Out of nowhere, Obama raised $125 million dollars a year before the general election, crushing his democratic opponents in fundraising. The average donation Obama received was just under $80. Obama and his online team showed that the ability to quickly and safely donate small amounts online was a powerful force. The iChurch can now harness that powerful force.

It is very simple to add a free donation program (we will refer to them as "modules") such as paypal.com or kimbia.com to your website to collect money online. With this program, a website user can easily select their own amount and donate in seconds using a credit card. Your ministry, however, must still pay the credit card processing fees for handling the transaction. There are also donation programs/modules where an online user can set up automatic recurring withdrawals from their bank account or credit card to give to the church.

eChecks are yet another way for users to pay/donate online. eChecks are payments that you make directly from your bank account. Note that the ability to use debit cards for online donations is not easily done for free at this time so that feature is not prominent in eCommerce.

For some, the convenience factor is a big reason for iChurch online donations. The younger generation is very familiar with donating online. In fact, many young people have never written a check but they are very familiar with online shopping (or donations) from their computer or mobile devices and using a credit card online. If you add a mobile component to the iChurch such as "text to give" or a mobile website/app with online donation capabilities, you can harness the power of impulse donations. When a person is at an event where your church is represented, with a mobile module as part of your iChurch, that person can donate right there as the spirit moves them instead of having to drive home, log on to their computer and then donate. This may be hours later.

Another feature is record keeping. These online donations modules give an instant receipt to the person donating which is often very important to them. For the church, this also saves staff time months later because these online donation modules keep records for the church such as who donated, how much they donated and when they donated. This information is important for the ministry's financial records.

An online donation eCommerce module added to your website can collect a large amount of money from online users, many of whom may never set foot in your church. These online users may donate smaller amounts, as Obama showed, but volume, not size, is what counts.

Online Event Registration - This module creates the easiest way to get paid for an event. There are no bounced checks to deal with. It reduces the need for a large staff. It can distribute tickets and give receipts to the participants. You can set limits on attendance. It reduces calls and customer service. You can add details to the information the participant receives such as the date and time of the event, a map showing the location, parking instructions and whether or not daycare is provided. This module can also capture data from each participant that can be used to market products and services to them later. Typical data capture can include name, address, emails, phone numbers, age, gender and marital status. With an online event registration module, you should be able to increase the profit for each event.

Online Store - Adding an online store to the iChurch is a little bit different that the above items. Although you can set up an online store for free, most online store modules can cost up to $1,000. With an online store, you must have products or services to sell. Also, you want to make sure your online store has the same look as your website so the user doesn't feel like they have left your ministry brand. Here are some benefits of adding an online store to the iChurch.

Digital Products - These are all profit. There is no shipping, no handling, no staff, no storage fees and no product creation costs. Digital products can be podcasts, eBooks, documents or videos. The ordering system is easy for the online users. And they receive the product instantly so the iChurch can tap into the moment the spirit moves them. The purchaser is emailed a secure download link they click on to receive the product. This link is good for only 72 hours. The only downside is that the digital product is not protected or restricted so they *could* share it with someone else and you won't receive payment for that usage. On the plus side, this nonpayer will be exposed to your church or ministry. With this module, you can capture some information such as name, address and email addresses to use in later marketing plans. Selling digital products through an online store is a nice profit builder for the iChurch. I like the phrase: load once, fire forever!

Tangible products - For the iChurch, tangible products consist of items like books, cd's and DVD's. Although you still need staff to handle and ship the products, collecting money is made much simpler. And again, I can't overemphasize the component of impulse buying. If the buyer is at an event and has their mobile device, they can order the product now and pay for it even though they won't receive it for a few days.

Add On Features - With an online store module, you can add on features such as **online coupons**. A coupon often triggers the buyer to make a purchase they might not have otherwise. The iChurch can take advantage of that impulse. **Wishlists** are another nice feature allowing the potential buyer to create a list of items they want to purchase at a later date, perhaps when you send them an online coupon. **Product reviews** can be added to allow the online buyer the opportunity to tell everyone about the experience with their purchase. Good reviews often trigger more sales.

Mobile Browser Support – Let's jump ahead to Part 5 real quick. When someone wants to access your website from a mobile device, the experience is not pleasant....unless you have a mobile browser. You may have experienced it when you access a website on your laptop or computer and see a full, robust website. Then, you access the same website from your mobile device and the website looks different and it's easy to use too. That's because the company has set up two websites: one for traditional computers and one for mobile devices. Adding a mobile browser support for your online store makes the experience much more pleasant for the online user. And again, the iChurch can take advantage of location and impulse. So long as the person has their mobile device with them, they can buy or donate anywhere, anytime. This is called mCommerce or Mobile Commerce. How big is mCommerce? PayPal recently stated it handles $10 million in mobile transactions each day! And that's just PayPal. If you want to take the iChurch to the next level, adding a mobile browser to your online store is a must. The easiest way to create a mobile online store is to purchase an online store that has a mobile component/add-on. The store should automatically convert to a mobile format when a user is viewing the online store from a mobile device. Here is an example of a regular online store viewed on a mobile device versus a mobile optimized store viewed from a mobile device. Online store examples such as www.aspdotnetstorefront.com, www.magentogo.com and www.virtuemart.net are mentioned in the tech talk section later in this Part.

Regular Online Store Website from a mobile phone

Mobile Optimized Online Store from a mobile phone

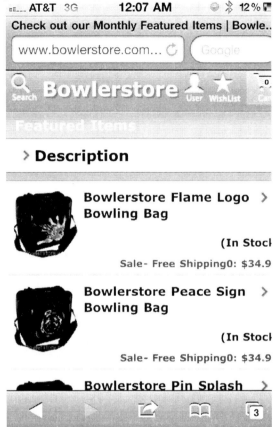

Social Commerce - Facebook is grabbing a tremendous share of online visitors (750 million), especially younger people. Placing your online store on Facebook or other social media is a great idea to not only increase revenue but reach these different age groups. The iChurch should always place its store where people are at. Social media is where they are at. And Facebook is the leader in social media. Facebook has proved itself as a viable platform on which to place an online store. The easiest way to create a Facebook online store is to purchase an online store module that has a Facebook component/add-on. The purchased store should automatically convert your online store to a Facebook friendly format when a user is viewing your store from Facebook.com. Here is an example of a Facebook store.

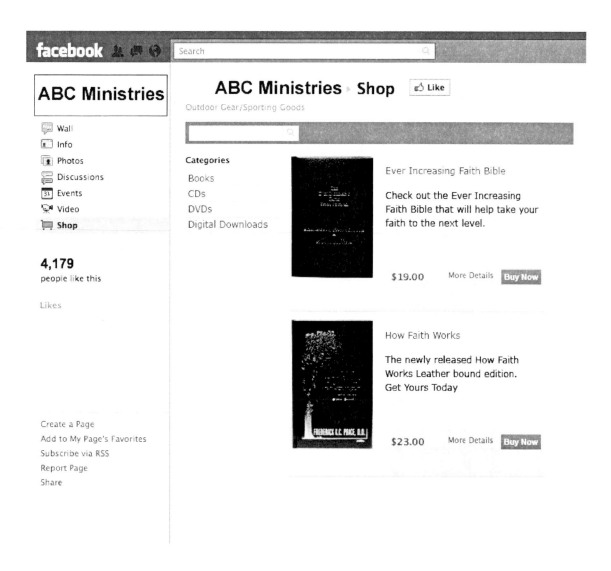

In summary, the iChurch needs money to survive and spread the good news. Money comes from supporters. eCommerce is the vehicle to deliver what God has given to the supporters for your iChurch.

What I Want For My iChurch - Part 3

(a) I want eCommerce on my website.

(b) I want an online donation module for my website that can:

    1. Accept credit Cards.

    2. Accept eChecks.

    3. Provide great record-keeping ability.

    4. Capture information about the givers.

(c) I want an online event registration module for my website that will:

    1. Accept payment.

    2. Issue tickets.

    3. Capture information about the purchasers.

    4. Provide a map to the event.

    5. Provide details about the event.

(d) I want an online store for my website that can:

    1. Sell digital products.

    2. Sell tangible products.

    3. Allow coupons to be sent.

    4. Establish wish lists.

    5. Allow for product reviews.

    6. Comes with a mobile browser.

    7. Places the store on Facebook.

Let's Talk Tech

How to setup a PayPal account for online donations and online stores

The first step in establishing any type of online eCommerce option for your ministry, whether it be online donations, online registrations with payment and/or an online store is to create a merchant account that people can use to pay you. The most common one is Paypal.com. I also believe that kimbia.com is a great way to accept money online but their setup process is more involved than PayPal. PayPal has established itself as the easiest way to accept money online and most online users are familiar and comfortable with using them. So, let's walk through the process of setting up a PayPal account for the iChurch and creating an online donation button.

Step 1: Go to Paypal.com. If you don't have an account, then you need to set one up by clicking on "Sign Up" right beneath the yellow "Log In" button. If you already have an account, then login and skip to step 5. Otherwise, go to step 2.

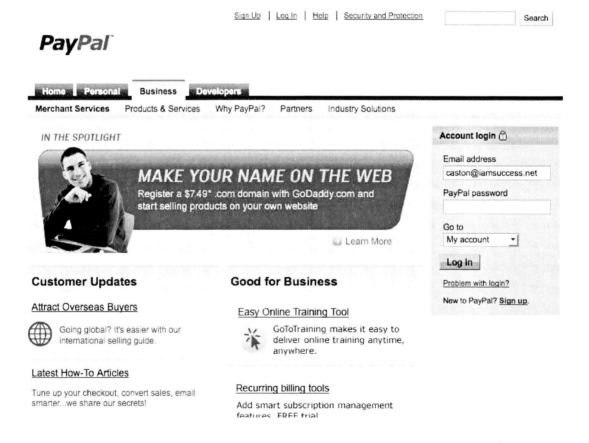

Step 2: After clicking on the "Sign Up" link, you will get the screen below. Choose your country or region, your language and then click the yellow "Get Started" button under **Business** account.

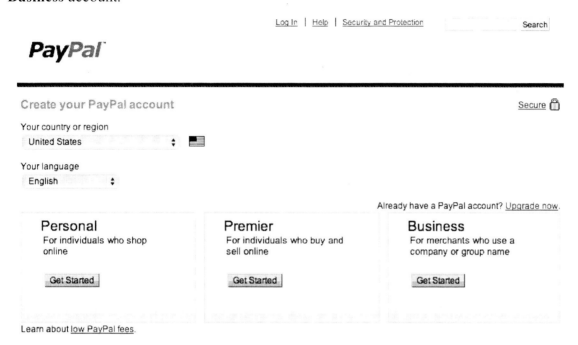

Step 3: Next, you will need to choose your payment solution. For now, we will start with the **Website Payments Standard.** This is a good solution to start with. Once the ministry is established with this account then we can look at moving up to the **Website Payments Pro** solution.

Step 4: Now you need to fill in your ministry information and setup a password. You will also need to add a bank account to the PayPal account so they can put your online transactions into a bank account. Fill out the information below as well as the next screen. PayPal will explain what needs to be done to verify your bank account. Once you have completed that step, you will be ready to login and use PayPal for your ministry.

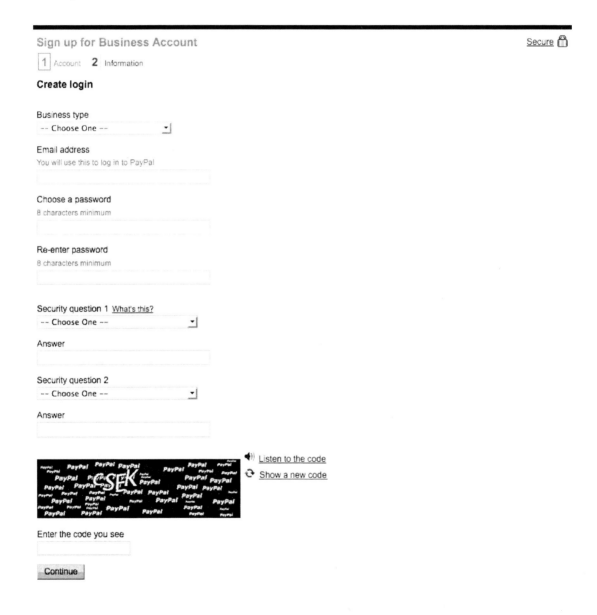

Step 5: Once you are logged into your account, you need to click on the **Merchant Services** tab at the top of the page.

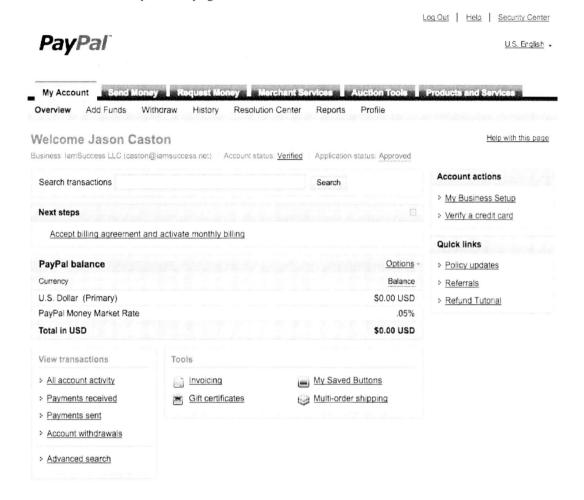

Step 6: When you get to the **Merchant Services** screen, you need to click the **Donate link** in the **Create Buttons** column. The **Donate link** is outlined below so that you can find it easily.

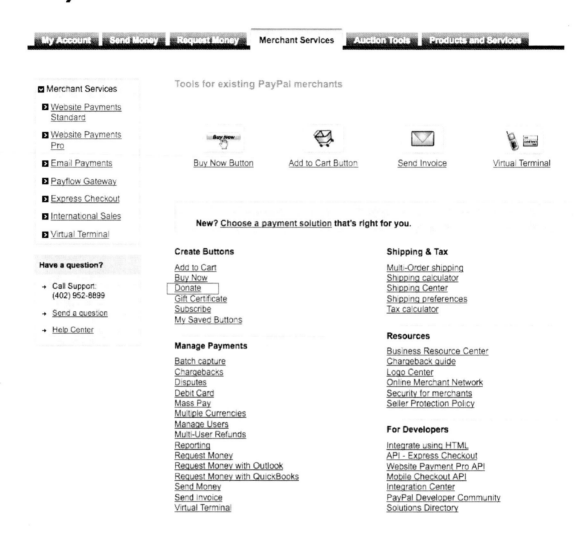

Step 7: Choose a button type ("**Donations**"), and then put your ministry name into the "**Organization name/service**" box. The "**Donation ID**" box can be left blank unless you want a donation sku for your records. In the Customize button area, you can click on the "**Customize text or appearance**" link and choose the look of your yellow "**Donate**" button. Once you have completed that, you can choose whether you want the donors to enter a fixed amount or choose any amount they want to donate (I suggest that you let them enter their own amount). Finally, leave the "**Use my secure merchant account ID**" option selected and click **Step 2: Save your buttons (optional).**

Create PayPal payment button

PayPal payment buttons are an easy way to accept payments. Check the Website Payments Standard Overview for more information.

Use this page to customize your button and create the HTML you'll need to copy and paste into your website. Learn more

Having trouble viewing this page?

▼ **Step 1: Choose a button type and enter your payment details**

Choose a button type   (i) Which button should I choose?

Donations   ▼

Note: Go to My saved buttons to create a new button similar to an existing one.

Organization name/service   Donation ID (optional)   What's this?

Customize button   **Your customer's view**

▶ Customize text or appearance (optional)

Donate

[VISA] VISA [cards] [BANK]

Currency

USD ▼

Contribution amount

⦿ Donors enter their own contribution amount.
○ Donors contribute a fixed amount.

Merchant account IDs Learn more

⦿ Use my secure merchant account ID
○ Use my primary email address caston@iamsuccess.net

▶ Step 2: Save your buttons (optional)

▶ Step 3: Customize advanced features (optional)

Create Button

Step 8: On this screen, check the "**Save button at PayPal**" so that you can keep this button for future use on another website or in case you misplace the code for this button. Then, click the "**Step 3: Customize advanced features (optional)**."

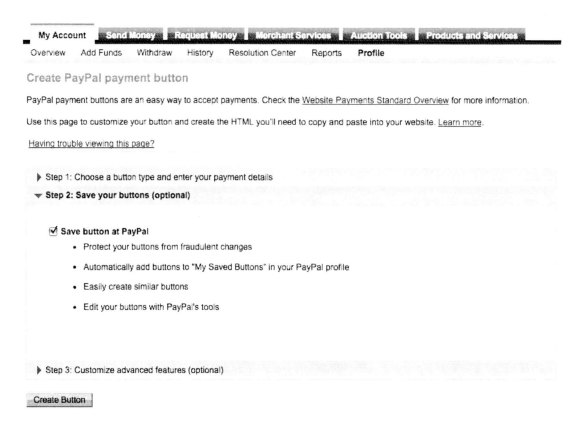

Step 9: Leave the default options in place which are "**Can your customer add special instructions in a message to you? Yes**" and "**Do you need your customer's shipping address? Yes.**" Finally, leave the rest of the options blank unless you have a need for them and click the yellow "**Create Button.**"

▶ Step 1: Choose a button type and enter your payment details

▶ Step 2: Save your buttons (optional)

▼ **Step 3: Customize advanced features (optional)**

Customize checkout pages

If you are an advanced user, you can customize checkout pages for your customers, streamline checkout, and more in this section.

Can your customer add special instructions in a message to you?

⦿ Yes

Name of message box (40-character limit)

| Add special instructions to the seller |

○ No

Do you need your customer's shipping address?

⦿ Yes
○ No

☐ Take customers to this URL when they cancel their checkout

Example: https://www.mystore.com/cancel

☐ Take customers to this URL when they finish checkout

Example: https://www.mystore.com/success

Advanced variables What's this?

Use a line break between each variable. The variables will appear in your button's HTML code. Learn more

☐ Add advanced variables

Example
address_override=1
notify_url=https://www.mywebsite.com/PayPal_IPN

Create Button

Step 10: Take the code that PayPal generated for your donation button and put it on your website where you want the donation button to appear. Once an online user clicks the button, they will be able to donate to your ministry via PayPal. You may need some technical help to place the code on your website.

Setup an online store

There are a variety of options that a ministry can use to setup an online store. We won't walk you through the process of setting up an online store because each store is different. What we will do is give you the features of each store and let you decide which ones are best for your ministry.

MagentoGo - http://go.magento.com/ - an online store that helps ministries build a powerful store to sell products and services, quickly and easily. With Magento Go, there is no software to install or configure and no servers to manage. They handle the technology so you can focus on running and growing your online business. The key elements of Magento Go, according to their website, are Customizable Design, Unlimited Product Options, Customer Retention and Loyalty, and Customer

Engagement. To start using Magento Go you simply go to their website and click "Try Magento Go for Free." They will give you a 30-day FREE trial.

Listed below are the features and drawbacks of using Magento Go for your online store:

- Benefits
    - Hosted solution that doesn't have to be maintained and can be setup for you for as little as $15 per month.
    - Customizable themes so you can match your store to the look of your website.
    - Online Gift Cards.
    - Online Coupons.
    - Reporting features.
    - Social Media integration where people can share products on Facebook and Twitter.
    - Wishlist features.
    - Customizable Shipping options (free shipping, etc.).
    - One Page Checkout.
    - PayPal integration.
    - Upgrades automatically.
- Drawbacks
    - No digital downloads at the current time.
    - No mobile theme compatibility at the current time.

Aspdotnetstorefront – http://www.aspdotnetstorefront.com - This is a storefront platform that absolutely offers the most features for the money. I am confident that your online ministry will be successful using this company. Aspdotnetstorefront has a hosted feature where you can setup an online store on their servers and not have to host it on your own web servers. This service costs $595 for up to 30 products. If you have more, the cost is significantly higher at $1,295. Again, this store is by far the best in terms of features and stability and the hosted version.

Listed below are the features and drawbacks of using this online store:

- Benefits
    - Hosted solution that doesn't have to be maintained and can be setup for you for as little as $15 per month.
    - Customizable themes so you can match your store to the look of your website.
    - Online Gift Cards.
    - Online Coupons
    - Reporting features.
    - Social Media integration where people can share products on Facebook and Twitter.
    - Wishlist features.
    - Customizable Shipping options (free shipping, etc.).
    - One Page Checkout.
    - Mobile add-on (for $25 per month).
    - Facebook Store add-on ($500 onetime fee).
    - Digital downloads.
    - PayPal integration.
    - Upgrades automatically add-on ($120 one-time fee).
- Drawbacks
    - High entry costs.
    - More difficult to setup unless you use hosted option.

Virtuemart – http://www.virtuemart.com - VirtueMart is an Open Source eCommerce solution to be used together with a Content Management System (CMS) called Joomla!. This is an online store that you can either host on your own servers or purchase website hosting to install on their servers.

Listed below are the features and drawbacks of using this online store:

- Benefits
    - o Mobile friendly with Joomla! Mobile add-on.
    - o Customizable themes so you can match your store to the look of your website.
    - o Online Gift Cards.
    - o Online Coupons.
    - o Reporting features.
    - o Customizable Shipping options (free shipping, etc.).
    - o Digital downloads.
    - o PayPal integration.
    - o Low costs - FREE.
- Drawbacks
    - o Open source solution that has to be maintained and secured by you.
    - o Can become unstable.
    - o You have to manually upgrade this software.
    - o Is dependent on Joomla! CMS.

Part 4
Social Media for Ministry: Engage and Connect

Let's Talk Strategy

What is Social Media?

Social Media is a broad topic with a broad range of explanations. Numerous people have branded themselves as social media experts and if you did a search for Social Media on Google you would find millions of websites with different explanations for this growing topic. My goal with this book is to give a general understanding of social media in the broad sense but a specific explanation on how to use it for your ministry. There are numerous statistics, facts and definitions that people quote when talking about social media but when it comes to social media and ministry, the consensus is simple, **interactive communication reaching the masses**. Another part of the Great Commission.

So how did social media come about? When the first website was born, the programmer placed words on a screen. That was all he could do. An online user could read the words but do nothing else much like a passing motorist viewing a billboard. As time marched on, email accounts were added to websites which allowed the online user to email the website owner. If the website owner and the user desired, they could carry on a conversation through email exchanges. This process was slow, but interactive nonetheless.

As people desired more instantaneous communications, various services were born such as instant messaging and texting. Soon, people were exchanging messages without the need to email. But people wanted to share photos and other content and still communicate instantly. Boom! Social Media was born. Think facebook and Twitter, then mix in YouTube with Wordpress and you have instant communication with user-generated content. Today, these social media sites have over <u>one billion</u> registered users and are free to join. Social media sites have changed the way users use the internet.

So before we end this section, let's answer the question "What is Social Media?" Social Media is having interactive digital conversations and generating interactive digital content and multimedia amongst online users around the world.

<u>Why is Social Media important in The iChurch Method?</u>

With information spreading fast from one friend to another, if your church is the one controlling the message, that's a good thing. People will talk no matter what so it's imperative for your church to be involved and participate in the conversation. Also, social media is the easiest marketing channel that a ministry can use. A great iChurch should take advantage of this and have a social network outreach ministry that reaches people outside of your website, interacts and communicates with them, and hopefully brings them back to the website for more information. Let's look at the key reasons why social media is important to the iChurch.

<u>More People</u> - Social media reaches far more people than anything else out there. The key feature with Facebook is that a posting of content on Person A's page (wall) alerts all of his friends to the new information and sends some or all of that new information to these friends. It is a like a mass email without you having to take any action other than posting content on your Facebook page. When Person A's friends receive this mass email, they can spread it to their friends which is likely a different group than Person A's friends. This process goes on and on especially with compelling content. Have you heard the phrase, "going viral?" Compelling content can spread so fast on social media that computer servers often shutdown due to the high volume.

<u>Interactive</u> - Another reason why social media is critical to the iChurch is the interactive feature. Being able to have and maintain a two-way conversation allows for dozens of possibilities for the iChurch. Is someone thinking about becoming a Christian? Or considering attending your church? Perhaps they are depressed. Or sick. Have they recently lost a loved one and need counseling? Are they looking to volunteer with your church? Social media allows for instant responses and continued communication with

relevant content such as video, photos and podcasts. And I really want to emphasize the *immediacy* of the connection. If a staff member is assigned to this task, they will be able to respond faster which makes the chances of helping the other person greater.

Reach - Still yet another reason for using social media for the iChurch is the *reach*. With reach, social media can extend the iChurch to members farther away in other countries. This is a huge advantage especially with missionary work all over the world bringing new people to Christianity each day. The reach of social media extends the iChurch to the mobile phone which is the only asset many people in foreign countries possess. Imagine what the Apostles could have done with social media.

Direct Connection and Access - Access to church leadership is important to many members. Social media allows for this to happen. Church leadership can decide how they will connect to members and what information members receive. Social media also allows for simple and effective connections to ministries, which in turn provides greater interest, participation and financial support.

Branding - Using social media networks to get the word out about your church allows you to brand it. Branding is important because it helps people understand what your church stands for. It also aids greater participation in church events and increased church membership. Another benefit of branding is the sale of more products as people connect with your brand more intimately. Many books have been written on the importance of branding. With social media, you can create and maintain your brand.

eCommerce - Social media networks make it easy to add eCommerce and thus, generate revenue online through donations. Displaying the progress of the latest fund raising goals can turn these online users into online givers. To sell church products, online stores can be set up and integrated with social media to generate more revenue and of course, add a greater iChurch presence.

Research - Social media is an excellent tool for engaging customers and church members in a dialogue and asking their input on particular issues. Because it is easy to give feedback, users have a higher rate of participation in questionnaires and quality control surveys. If your church is trying to decide on a particular matter, creating a survey on a social media site will provide all the feedback and opinions you need to reach a decision.

Customer Retention/Service - Being able to answer questions from your members and online users creates a high satisfaction rating. This in turn maintains a higher retention rate for your church. Using social media to address your member's issue before it becomes a big problem is critical because social media can spread negative information as fast as it spreads positive information.

Lead Generation - Social media allows your church to actively seek out new members by searching through tweets and Facebook pages to find people with special talents or someone struggling with a certain issue. Promotions are another way you can bring in new members or customers. And a promotion is easy to set up on a social media site.

Share Everything! – Sharing everything doesn't necessarily mean pulling back the veil and letting everyone into every aspect of your ministry. But there are two important concepts of sharing that Social Media provide. First, share as much content as possible via your social networks. Share daily inspirations, weekly events, ministry updates, weekly sermons, products, leadership updates, photos, videos, blogs and everything else you can think of that would be of interest to members, potential members and online supporters. This continuous flow of fresh content keeps your social networks vibrant and gives your online users lots of information to consume and re-share. Second, make as much content shareable as possible. When you post content to your social networks, it's automatically shareable by the networks. When you post this content to your website, you can add Facebook Like buttons, Google +1 buttons and Sharethis sharing links so that users can share your content with their social networks right from your website. This makes your content shareable so no matter what a user is reading on your website, they can immediately share it with their networks.

When you ask, "What can social media do for my iChurch?" the answer is, "Just about everything!"

Social Media Strategy - What strategy should the iChurch have for social media?
The answer is "a consistent one." This is also the most difficult part of using social media. Too many times a company or church will lay out a consistent social media

strategy but find the time commitment to maintain that strategy is more than the staff has available. Another difficult hurdle to a consistent social media strategy is producing consistent content. So what can we do to set up a social media strategy that works for your iChurch?

First, you must look at your staff and decide how much time they can devote to a social media strategy. Be realistic. Make sure you understand what tasks each person already performs and ensure these new duties can fit time wise into their new responsibilities. Next, look at the content you currently generate. In previous Parts, we mentioned and explained repurposing content. Social media is an excellent use for repurposed content. Take a careful inventory of your weekly production of content and make a list of how many different items your staff can produce. Content is king. If you have plenty of staff and time to post to social media sites yet have poor or inconsistent content, the effectiveness of the iChurch is greatly diminished.

Notice how I haven't stated whether to use Facebook, Twitter, YouTube or any other social media network yet. The network that you push content out to your online users is irrelevant if there isn't a consistent strategy behind it. Ten years ago, everyone was using AOL email to communicate with the masses. Five years ago it was MySpace. Three years ago Facebook and Twitter became popular. Just recently, Google+ has been introduced to the masses. The networks will come and go but the strategy remains the same: make sure the content from your ministry flows consistently via your online properties to your online users. With all that in mind, here is a strategy I recommend to you and your church.

How to manage it all:

- How many staff? - The first question that a ministry needs to answer is how many people will participate in the social media strategy of the ministry. My recommendation is that you have two people to start out and see how that goes. The reason that I suggest two people is that one person should be in charge of gathering content for the ministry and the other person should be in charge of pushing it out. Of course you can have more people do this because you may want to have people commenting and responding to users on the social networks. But initially, the main focus is gathering content and pushing it out.

- How many hours per day? – Social media operates 24 hours a day. However, it's unrealistic to believe that someone will be managing your social media properties for the ministry 24 hours a day. Instead, dedicate 2 – 4 hours daily gathering content, scheduling it for social networks and responding to online users. As time progresses and you get more people involved on behalf of the ministry, you will increase those hours. Hopefully though, your process will be much more streamlined.

- Software to help – Hootsuite.com is scheduling software that is free to use and makes social media management much easier. Hootsuite connects with social networks Facebook and Twitter and allows you to schedule updates, add files and coordinate a full social media strategy from one location. The main benefit of Hootsuite is that you can schedule out all your Facebook and Twitter posts for the week (or month) at one time and let the software automatically post items for you. This will keep a continuous stream of content coming from the ministry and allow you to focus on other things such as gathering more content or responding to online users from various social networks.

When to Post

Another important question in the social media strategy is "when to post?" Since social media operates 24 hours a day, you cannot assume that all of your online users are only within your city, state or time zone. Therefore, you must adjust and adapt your social media strategy to a 24-hour schedule. This doesn't mean that someone has to be up at 2 a.m. posting for the ministry. When using Hootsuite.com, your content is already scheduled for posting. You can simply schedule overnight posts for people that may be on your social networks during late hours or on the other side of the world where it's daytime while you are sleeping. Here are some example posting times:

- First Post - Early morning 6 a.m. - 10 a.m.
- Second Post - Late Morning 10 a.m. - 12 p.m.

- Third Post - Early Afternoon 12 p.m. - 3 p.m.
- Fourth Post - Late Afternoon 3 p.m. - 5 p.m.
- Fifth Post - Evening 5 p.m. - 9 p.m.
- Sixth Post - Overnight 9 p.m. - 6 a.m.

Post at least two to three times each day, preferably in the early morning, early afternoon and evening. Those times are most ideal. If you can generate more posts, then you can fill the overnight and early morning slots.

Content and Multimedia Types to Post

There are a several types of content we can post via social networks. Ranging from just plain text to a full video, we can put out just about anything via our social networks and use this content to reach the masses. Listed below are the numerous types of content that we can distribute on Facebook, Twitter, Blogs, LinkedIn, Google+, YouTube and other social networks.

- Video – Videos are the most engaging form of multimedia. They can be created from devices such as professional cameras to Flip Video Cameras. Once the video is recorded and edited, it can be uploaded to numerous social media websites.
- Links – Links are simply text you can click on. Once clicked, these links can take you to videos, documents, audio files, websites, images or online posts such as blogs.
- Statuses – A status update is a text-based update that is informational. Some social networking sites have character limits such as Facebook (5000 characters) and twitter (140). Facebook has a feature for posts that are longer than 5000 characters. They are called "Notes" and these can be as long as you desire.
- Photos – Photo updates are one of the most popular uses of social networks. Since you can take pictures from 90% of smart phones these days, millions of people are taking photos and sharing them via social networks. Remember to only post images you own or have permission to post.
- Questions/Polls – Questions and Polls were originally just a status post that asked a question and waited for people to respond. Now, in Facebook there is a specific

question/poll feature where you can ask a question and the feature will automatically allow your fans or friends to answer while you see the results in real time.

- Events – In Facebook, you can setup events, invitations and reminders that people can RSVP to online. This online events feature provides the same functionality as a service such as evite and lets you see who is coming to your event as well as letting people share and socialize about your event.

- Location based strategies (check-in feature) – The newest feature that has been quite popular is location based social networking. Foursquare, Facebook and twitter have features where you can broadcast your location to your friends. Another option is the check-in feature where users can "check-in" to places via their mobile devices and in addition to broadcasting their location, they can receive online coupons and deals.

Ministry Content You Should Post

Now that we have discussed the forms of content posting, let's talk about specific ministry content that you can post. The ministry produces a variety of content and once you start to gather it and repurpose it, you can distribute it through a variety of social networks. Here are some examples of great ministry content that can be sent out via social networks.

- Products – Links to products in the online store can be sent out via social networks. Your online fans can then find out about sales, promotions and hot products that the ministry is offering.

- Pastoral/Leadership Updates – Videos, Blogs and other quick updates can help your social media followers feel connected to the pastor and leadership. It doesn't have to be a professionally produced video or an award winning novel. Just give the users a way to connect with the pastor and/or leadership via the social networks.

- Photos – Keep those photos coming!! Make sure to distribute photos of church worship and activities, community work and new staff members. There's a variety of things that you can take pictures of and distribute via your social networks, so make sure you keep those photos coming!!

- Daily Inspiration – Each day, people are looking for some type of hope, motivation and inspiration from their spiritual leaders. A word from the pastor could start many followers' day off with hope and joy. You can also encourage them throughout the day with more posts.

- Video clips from TV shows – Every week, the ministry TV show is aired. There are commercial video clips that could help increase awareness, interest and viewership of the weekly show. In addition to showing the video clips of the TV show, the actual show could be shown online using vimeo.com and a custom landing page tab, with a link to donate online during the show.

- Video clips from Sunday service – Each week, the church shows multimedia clips during the service. These clips and previous sermons can be posted online. Previous sermons could also be made into clips and distributed via Facebook.

- Live service – When the church starts offering a live service, they can update users online when it is service time and start to build their online service audience around service times such as Saturday at 6pm and Sunday at 9:30am and 11am.

- Interactive Polls – In order to get online users talking and interacting with the Facebook fan page (and other social media networks), weekly interactive polls that are ministry-based events, sermon topics and current events can be posted online. Results can be calculated instantly and shared among the Facebook fans.

- Weekly Reminders about the TV show – Each week, make sure to keep your social media fans updated on the day and times that the weekly ministry television show (online or network) airs. If the show is not online, make sure it is added to your social networks or website so that they can watch it from their computer and/or mobile devices.

- Weekly Reminders about Sunday service and the current series – Each week keep your social media fans connected by updating them on the church service times, the sermon series and the speaker.

- Weekly Reminders about the numerous events going on at Church – Each week keep your social media fans connected by updating them on the numerous events going on at the church.

- Saturday and Sunday posts about church service and weekend updates – A major posting strategy is to post updates (inspirational, events, etc.) on the weekend. Many churches post information about Sunday service over the weekend but they do not post the weekly information that followers enjoy such as daily inspiration, video links and other things that could help followers stay engaged not only during the week but on the weekend as well.

- Digital Downloads – Find a digital download to give away as incentive for online users to join the social media account. Make it a very inspiring message from the pastor that is selling well in the online store. This will make users feel like they are getting a high value product.
- Custom Tabs for Facebook – Create a custom welcome tab that has a download as an incentive. Also make sure the welcome tab highlights relevant ministry information such as an upcoming event, a welcome video, a featured product, a donation link, service times or any other relevant ministry information.

A Look At Some Social Media Sites

There are numerous social media websites and it would take me quite a long time to focus on them all. So, I will focus only on the major ones. These are the ones you hear about the most and the ones that seem to have the most users. I know that I will leave out some good ones (such as Tumblr.com) but that is only due to the fact that they have not yet had enough ministries registered to give me a chance to measure the impact of their service in terms of ministry.

Facebook - This is the by far the biggest social media site today. It has over 800 million registered users and is growing daily. Each day there are over 90 million status updates, which translate to a lot of usage. Updates have been increased to 5000 characters, which is significantly more than the 420 characters they were restricted to previously. Updates can be text, photos, videos, links, polls and pretty much whatever a person is doing on the internet. Facebook has two types of pages a user can set up. One is a profile page. This is where a user posts information about their day, their life and their friends. When a user makes a post to their profile page, his or her friends see what was added and can comment on it. Most recently, profile pages have been updated with the "subscribe" feature, where users can post "Public" for all "subscribed" users to see and comment. Another page a user can setup are Fan pages. A fan page displays a business, organization, brand, product, artist, band or cause. Churches usually have a fan page. Users of Facebook can become a fan of the fan page and receive information and changes when they are posted.

What's the difference between a Facebook profile page and a fan page? The bottom line is profiles are now only for individuals and pages are for nonindividuals. Profiles and fan pages have different features. Here are some features of Profile pages:

- Profile pages have a limitation of 5000 friends.
- Profile pages have distinct privacy features and are only accessed if the profile owner "adds you as a friend."
- Profile pages have all the features of Facebook such as updating statuses, photos, links, videos, applications, groups, wall posts and other interactive elements.
- Profile pages do not have customizable tabs similar to fan pages.
- Profile pages are much more common on Facebook and are easily created from the facebook.com homepage by filling out a few boxes to get started.

On the other hand, fan pages (which are also known as business pages) have these rules and features:

- Businesses are only allowed to open pages NOT Profile pages. A business which opens a Profile page is in direct violation of the TOS.
- Business pages allow other users to become fans, but access by the business to the fans' individual Profile pages is limited.
- Business pages do not allow the ability to invite friends. In fact, business pages cannot maintain a friends list. They can only maintain a fan list.
- Business pages do allow updating of status (which gets shared with your fans).
- Business pages allow pictures, videos, discussion board, application, wall posts, groups and other interactive elements.
- Business pages allow customization of tabs to promote interactivity.

The key to getting people to follow a Facebook user are: (a) post often, (b) make status updates, (c) upload videos and photos, (d) use polls, and (e) provide links to other sites and information.

Here are the best types of content to post on Facebook in descending order:

1. Video.
2. Status updates with Links.
3. Status updates with just text [inspirational quotes, words of wisdom, etc.].
4. Photos.
5. Questions/Polls.
6. Events.

Facebook is the leader among social media sites. With Facebook, a user can sign into their account, post a status that says they are in a happy mood today and everyone who has "friended" them (become members of their particular page) or "subscribed" to them, will see the status and can respond back leaving their own messages, photos or videos. That's Social Media. It allows for instant interaction between users. It also allows a user to read and react to another user's content. With Social Media, Person A can follow the events of Person B's day as well as Person B's other friends. Information flows fast like a gossip grapevine in a small town.

How can Facebook help your ministry? With over 800 million people on Facebook and a variety ways to send out ministry content, this is one of the best ways to take ministry to the people. Since many people are on Facebook, as long as the ministry is there, interacting and keeping the flow of content fresh, people will respond accordingly.

Twitter - Twitter is a service that allows a user to send out very short messages, 140 characters or less. It works on a similar principle as Facebook in that a user sets up an account and people can follow it. It's like standing on a hill and shouting out a message to the village below. As long as someone has selected the message giver's account to follow, they will receive the message. Twitter can gain a large number of followers quickly because the messages are so short recipients don't mind receiving them. With over 200 million users and over 70 million tweets a day, the audience is ready to listen and often, interact.

How can Twitter help your ministry? You need to get people to follow your twitter account. The key is to tweet often with great content. You can also take other users' tweets and retweet them. And you can tweet links to content you like as well as send multimedia and photos. Following other users may bring you more followers when the users decide to reciprocate and follow you. Interact. Take the ministry to the people and let them know that when they reach out to you via twitter, you will be there.

Google+ - Google+ is the newest social network and has rapidly increased its user base. It has functionality similar to Facebook with a few differences. As of the writing of this book, they have not yet released their business pages. So, it is currently *supposed* to be restricted to individuals only (I'm talking to you Coca-Cola and Ford with your Google+ pages). Here is one of the best things I have noticed about Google+. The potential integration with other apps and services that Google offers is tremendous. And Google+ was thinking mobile from day one. This long-term vision will help Google+ last far into the future. Here is a summary of my thoughts on Google:

- Business Profiles - Business profiles are coming within the next few months and depending on the number of features they have for marketing and interacting, they could be just as beneficial as Facebook fan pages. Google+ is currently deleting profiles that appear to be used for business purposes therefore they will either have a PR nightmare or their business pages will be so great that they make people forget this profile deleting fiasco. The benefit that Google+ has right now is that they can use Facebook profiles as a model and build a better social media site from that.

- Circles. Basically, this lets you organize the people you know into groups so you can communicate only with them. Friends, parents, co-workers and/or acquaintances can all go in different circles. Circles could be used by churches to organize different groups of people to whom to minister. For example, divorced recovery individuals could be assigned to a divorce recovery circle. If a ministry is setting up small groups online, they can use circles to setup which people will be in which group. This niche marketing tool could help the church focus different messages to different groups.

- Hangouts. Group video chat anyone? If multiple friends are online, you can all get together face-to-face. You can even watch YouTube videos together. This would take online ministry to another level by making ministry much more intimate and personal. Small groups can meet online via video chat and minister and fellowship with each other. If they decide not to use video chat then they could use messenger. This is group chat without the video.

I believe that Google+ has some great opportunities to help ministries make an impact online and you should really consider it.

YouTube – YouTube.com is the #1 site for video on the entire internet. It is the second largest search engine behind Google.com. YouTube is also owned by Google Inc. YouTube has 490 million registered users and millions more without an account. YouTube has more than 24 hours of video uploaded every minute. It gets two billion views per day. It also has 20 minute limit for most accounts (some accounts do not have the 20 minute limit) and is mobile device compatible (HTML5).

With these amazing stats, the question is: how can uploading ministry videos help your ministry? First and foremost, there are millions of viewers on YouTube.com everyday and you can tap into this audience by setting up your video page on YouTube.com. Of course, make sure you only put out content that you want the world to see and that reflects the ministry in a positive light. Keep in mind the content that comes from the church is supposed to be a beacon of light in this dark world. With millions of people on YouTube, there are sure to be millions that need the content the church and specifically your ministry has to offer. You may not have a video that goes viral every time you post something but if you reach just one person with a video and that helps them get saved, then the angels rejoice in heaven. Also, YouTube.com is free! That makes this type of marketing for your videos an amazing opportunity to get the visibility and word out about your ministry and attract new supporters both online and offline. You can let people comment on your videos, subscribe to your video page and become online friends with them so that you can communicate with your online audience and talk about your ministry videos. Finally, with every video that is uploaded to YouTube, you can get the code from them and embed these videos in your website so you can have a great multimedia presence. Great videos to put on YouTube are the same videos that we discussed earlier about posting on Facebook. Weekly sermons, ministry updates, product commercials and other videos that will help promote and advance your ministry online.

Foursquare - Location based social networking is rapidly becoming popular and Foursquare is leading the charge. Foursquare has done so well in helping people become comfortable with location based social networking that Twitter and Facebook copied the functionality and integrated it into their services. They say that imitation is the best form of flattery and Foursquare should be flattered. Many people were once wary of broadcasting their locations via social networks but Foursquare integrated badges (digital prizes) and let businesses offer coupons for people "checking in" at locations. Now everyone is checking in from all kinds of places including the North Pole, the South Pole and every place in between.

The question is: how can Foursquare help your ministry? Once you setup a Foursquare page for your ministry, you can give people incentives to "check in." These incentives can be coupons for products and other things. Each time someone "checks in," all of their friends on their Foursquare, twitter and Facebook social networks are notified and thus become online marketers for your location. This free marketing is a great opportunity for your ministry to attract new people.

To summarize, social media can spread the iChurch so fast, it is almost hard to comprehend. Your church or ministry must evaluate and consider establishing a social media strategy, even if you start very small. The returns on your investment in time will be huge.

What I Want For My iChurch - Part 4

(a) I want social media on my website to:

1. Reach more people.

2. Interact with followers.

3. Provide direct access to church leadership.

4. Branding my ministry or church.

5. Sell products through eCommerce.

6. Research.

7. Retain members and followers.

8. Lead generation.

9. Share and distribute the good news.

10. Location based check-ins.

11. Coupon and deals sent to check-ins.

(b) I want to post on social media the following items:

1. Daily inspirations.

2. Weekly events.

3. Service times.

4. Service locations and maps.

5. Ministry updates.

6. Videos.

7. Blog posts.

8. Weekly sermons.

9. Products for sale.

10. Leadership updates.

11. Photos.

12. Links.

13. Periodic status updates.

14. Question/Polls.

15. Bible passages.

16. Video clips of Sunday service.

17. Video of live service.

18. Audio of live service.

19. Reminders of Sunday service.

20. Updates regarding the current series.

21. Digital downloads.

(c) I want the following social media icons on my website to:

1. Facebook.

2. Twitter.

3. Sharethis.

4. Google+.

5. Foursquare.

(d) I want to set up Hootsuite.com to manage all of my social media postings.

(e) I want to post to my social media sites on the following schedule:

1. First Post - Early morning 6 a.m. - 10 a.m.

2. Second Post - Late Morning 10 a.m. - 12 p.m.

3. Third Post - Early Afternoon 12 p.m. - 3 p.m.

4. Fourth Post - Late Afternoon 3 p.m. - 5 p.m.

5. Fifth Post - Evening 5 p.m. - 9 p.m.

6. Sixth Post - Overnight 9 p.m. - 6 a.m.

(f) I want to set up custom tabs for facebook.

(g) I want to set up a fan page on facebook.

(h) I want to set up a custom twitter page.

(i) I want to set up a Google+ page (when it is allowable for businesses).

(j) I want to post videos to:

1. YouTube.

2. Vimeo.

3. Premium or Pro version of Vimeo.

(k) I want to set up a Foursquare page.

Let's Talk Tech

How to setup a Twitter account

1. Go to http://www.twitter.com and sign up for an account under the **New to Twitter?**

Box. Enter your Full Name, Email and Password and click the yellow button "Sign Up".

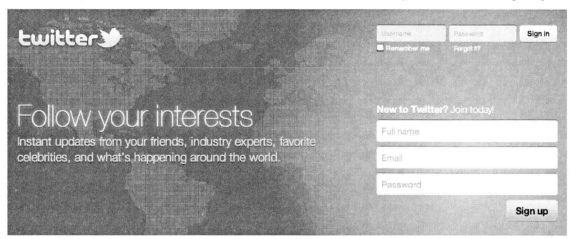

2. You will go to a page that has the information you just inserted so now you need to just choose a username and click the yellow button "Create My Account."

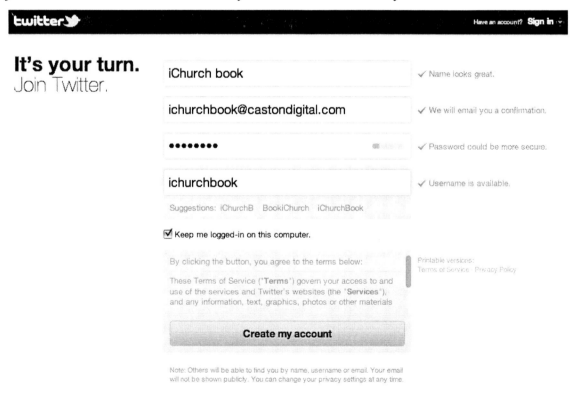

3. Unless you want to search your contact lists for the email providers and services listed, skip suggestions, skip interests and skip friends. Once you finally get to your twitter page as shown below, go to the top right and click on your username. Then go to settings tab.

Click on the "Profile" link and add a profile picture. Change your name if you want, update the location of your ministry, enter your ministry's website and insert a small bio about your church so that people can know this is the official ministry twitter page. Finally, click the blue button "save" and your page will be updated. Click the "Home" option on the black bar at the top of the page and you will get back to your twitter homepage. Now you can start tweeting.

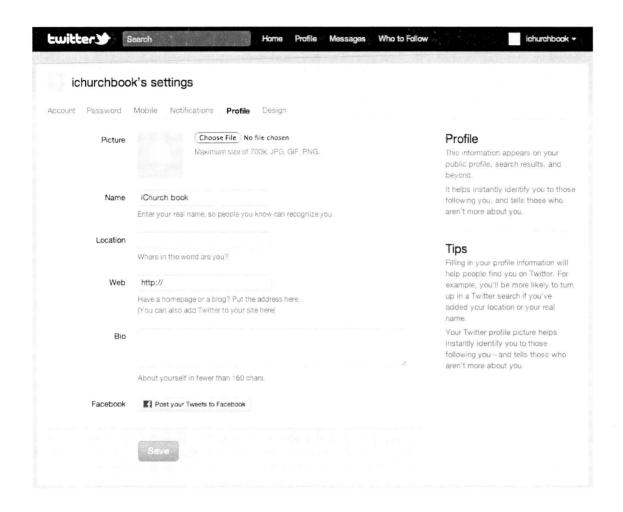

How to setup Facebook Profile account

1. Go to http://www.facebook.com and go to the boxes that are underneath the "Sign Up – It's free and always will be." Input your First Name, Last Name, Email, Email again, Password, Gender and Birthday. Once you have completed that, click the green button "Sign Up."

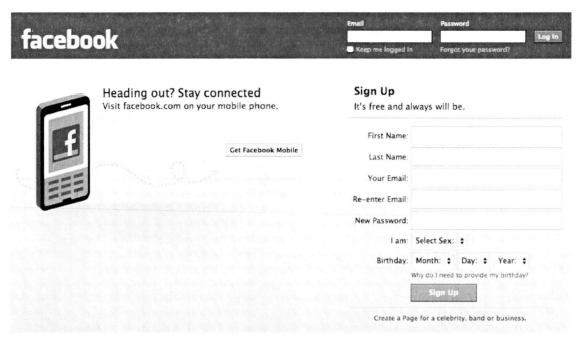

2. Click "Skip" on "Step 1 Find Friends" unless you want to search your contact lists for the email providers and services listed. Step 2 – Profile Information, add your Profile information such as High School, College and Employer. When you are done, click the blue button "Save & Continue."

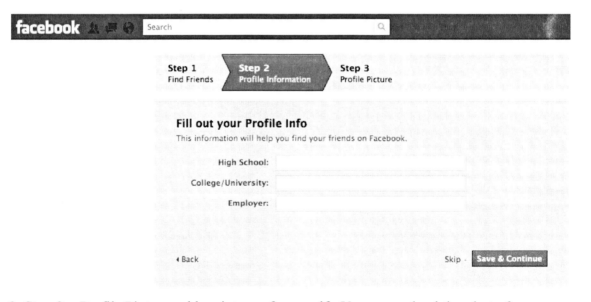

3. Step 3 – Profile Picture, add a picture of yourself. You can upload the photo from your computer or take a photo with your webcam. When you are done, click the blue button "Save & Continue."

4. Start using your new Facebook page. Once you have uploaded your picture and searched for people you may know, you can click the "News Feed" on the left and post your first status.

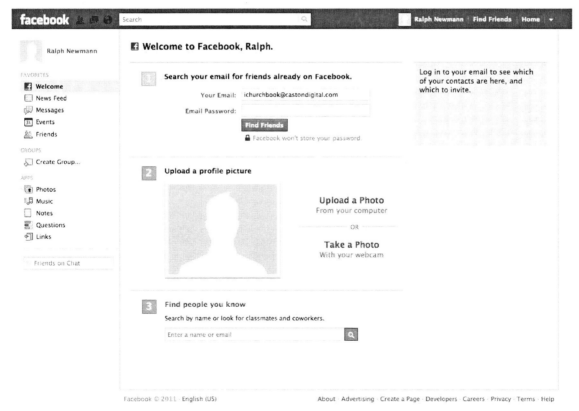

How to Create a Facebook Fan Page

1. Go to www.Facebook.com/pages and select the category your ministry falls under. The top choices are usually "Local Business or Place" or "Cause or Community." For this example we will use "Local Business or Place."

2. Choose a category that your ministry falls under from the dropdown menu. Next, type in the name of your ministry and the following lines which ask for the address and phone number. Finally, check the box "I agree to Facebook Pages Terms" and click on "Get Started."

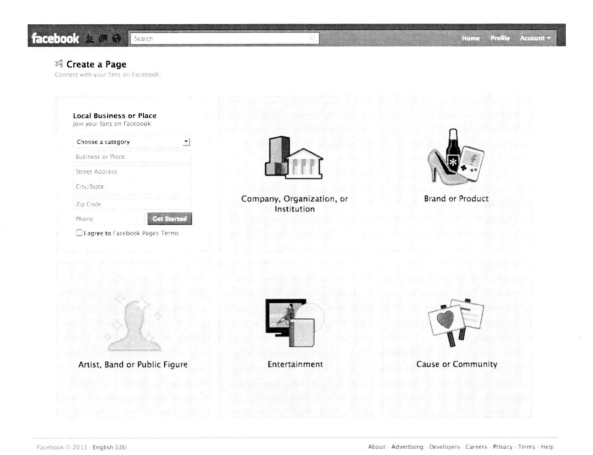

3. Now that you have created your fan page, let's start customizing it so that you can use it. Let's focus on the basics. Upload an image so that people can associate your fan page with some type of image. Your ministry logo is a great choice here.

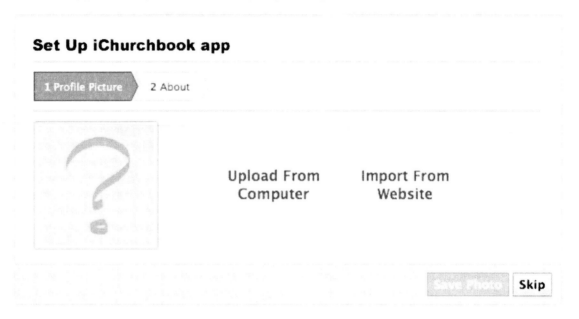

4. Next provide some basic information about your ministry as well as a link to your website. Once you are done click "Save Info"

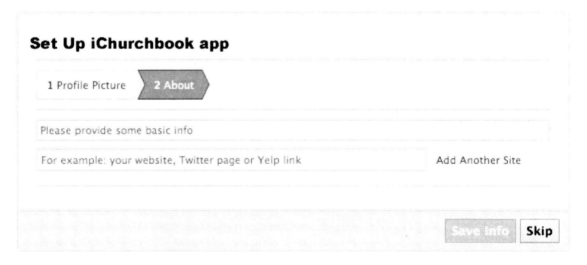

5. Now let's move onto setting up your new Facebook Timeline Fan Page. First make sure to like you new fan page, you are not only creating the page but you are the first fan. Congrats.

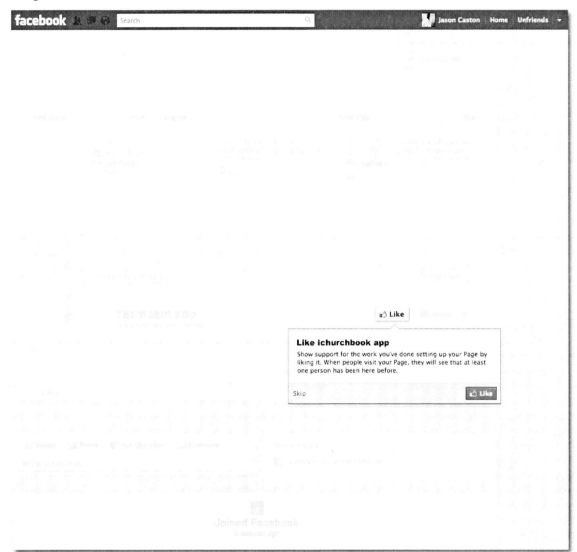

6. Next, invite your friends, import contacts from your church mailing list and start notifying people that this new fan page is available.

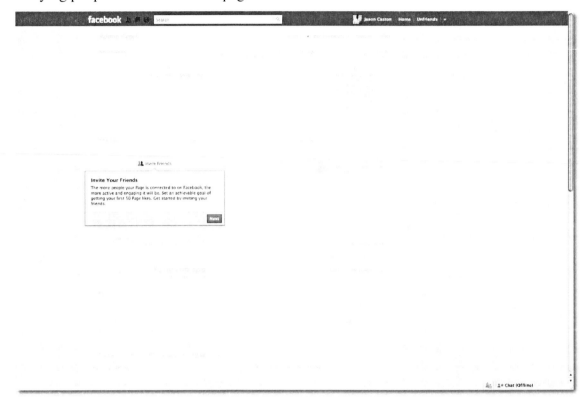

7. Post your first status letting people know that this page is live!!

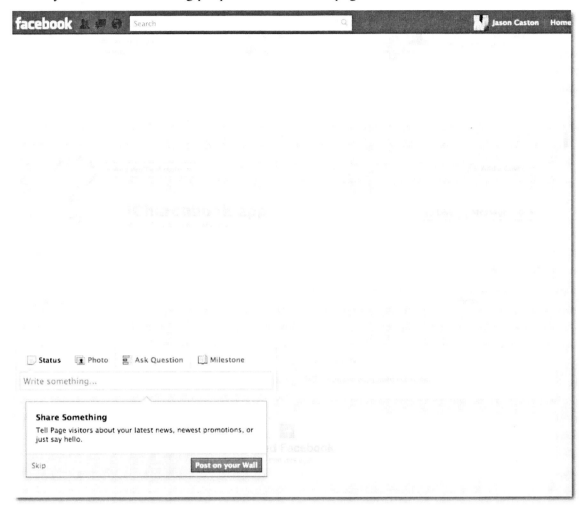

8. Now make sure to continue customizing your new page and don't forget to upload your cover image!!

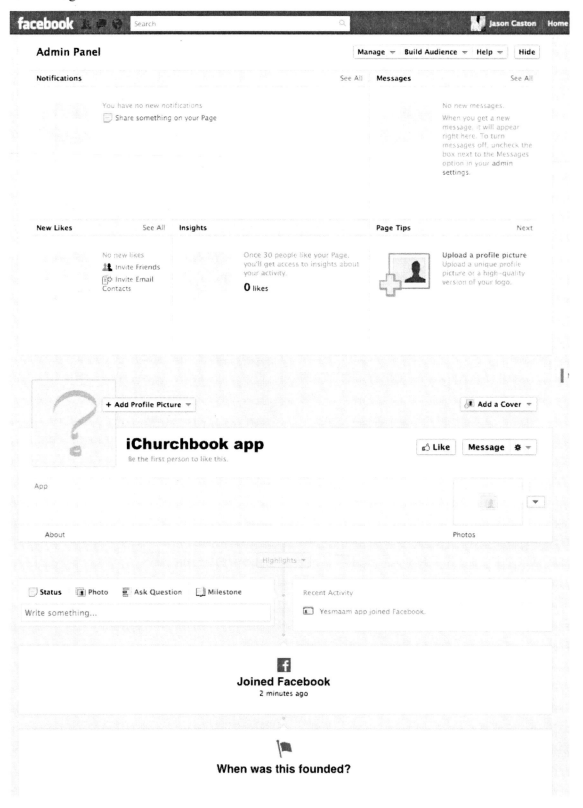

How to add a Facebook Like button to my website

Facebook has provided users with a way to notify their friends if they like a page when they are not on facebook.com. This is done with a Facebook like button. If you add the Facebook like button to your website, when people click it, they notify all of their Facebook friends that they "like" your page. There will be a link to your page posted in their news feed. Here is how you add the like button to your website.

1. Go to https://developers.facebook.com/docs/reference/plugins/like/ and you will see the page below. Fill in the box URL to Like (your website). Leave the Send Button box unchecked. Layout Style is "standard." Width can be "450" unless you want it smaller or larger. Leave the Show Faces box unchecked. Verb to display is "like." Color Scheme is "light" and Font is "Arial." Once you have done this, click the gray button "Get Code."

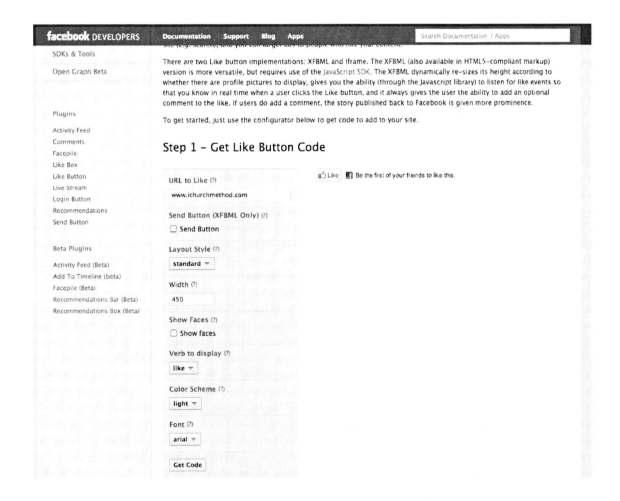

2. The box that pops up is your Facebook like button code. Take this code and put it into your website code. The like button will show up on your website for people to click and advertise for you.

How to add Google +1 button to my website

Google+ has provided users with a way to notify their friends if they like a page when they are not on facebook.com. This is done with a Google +1 button. If you add the Google +1 button to your website, when people click it, they notify all of their Google+ friends that they have "+1" your page. There will be a link to your page posted in their news feed. Here is how you add the +1 button to your website.

1. Go to http://www.google.com/webmasters/+1/button/ and you will see the page below. Fill in the information requested to get the code for your +1 button. Size can be left at "Standard (24px)." Annotation is "inline." Language can be "English" or changed to whatever language your website is in. Leave the advanced options alone for now. The code at the bottom has been updating itself as you were inputting options above so now that it is complete, copy and paste the code into your website.

Google +1 your website

 Add +1 to your pages to help your site stand out
Let visitors recommend your content on Google Search and share it on Google+

Customize your +1 button and +Snippet

+1 button preview

+1 | Jason Caston and 52549 others +1'd this

Size: ○ Small (15px)   ○ Medium (20px)
◉ Standard (24px)   ○ Tall (60px)

Annotation: inline ▾

Width: 450

Language: English (US) – English (US) ▾

⊞ Advanced options

Copy and paste the following code into your site:

```
<!-- Place this tag where you want the +1 button to render -->
<g:plusone annotation="inline"></g:plusone>

<!-- Place this render call where appropriate -->
<script type="text/javascript">
  (function() {
    var po = document.createElement('script'); po.type = 'text/javascript'; po.async = true;
    po.src = 'https://apis.google.com/js/plusone.js';
    var s = document.getElementsByTagName('script')[0]; s.parentNode.insertBefore(po, s);
  })();
</script>
```

How to place Addtoany/Sharethis buttons on my website so that I can share everything.

Addtoany.com and Sharethis.com are sharing buttons that allow you to share any page to your social networks. You can also share via email or save for later using a variety of services. Most people are familiar with Email, Facebook and Twitter for sharing, but Addtoany and Sharethis let you use other services that are not as popular such as Digg.com, Delicious.com and Stumbleupon.com. I prefer Addtoany.com over Sharethis but you can use either one. I will go through the single step to setup an Addtoany button and place it on your webpage.

1. Go to http://www.addtoany.com and click the big blue button that says "Get the Share Button." Once you click on that, you will get the page below. Now, let's input the information to get a code for your webpage. First, leave the type as "share/bookmark widget." Click the share option in the second row as we did below (the one with the icons for Facebook, twitter and email). Next, input the name of your page such as "Ministry homepage." Then input the URL of the page such as www.ministry.org. Finally, click the blue button "Get Button Code" and the code will popup below the button. Copy and paste that code into your webpage and you are done!!

Get the button

Type	Share/Bookmark Widget ⬍
Button	○ 🔲 Share / Save 🇫 📧 ⬍ ○ 🔲 Share / Save ⬍ More » ◉ 🔲 Share | 🇫 ✉ Customize...
Page name	[ ] Optional
Page url	[ ] Recommended

Get Button Code   More Options »

Or choose one of the following:

🅦 WordPress	🅦 WordPress.com
🔥 Drupal	🅑 Blogger (widget)
🇹 Tumblr	📋 TypePad (widget)
✖ Joomla	🔥 FeedFlare
🌐 Elgg	📦 Widgetbox

Next, let's look at the short process for sharethis.com. First, go to sharethis.com and

choose one of the popular button styles. Based on where you want the buttons to go on

your website, choose an option that will fit accordingly. I normally choose the third

option. Then click the "Get the Code" button.

Next fill out the registration form with your email address, domain name, and password. Click the "Register Button". Copy and paste that code into your webpage and you're done!!

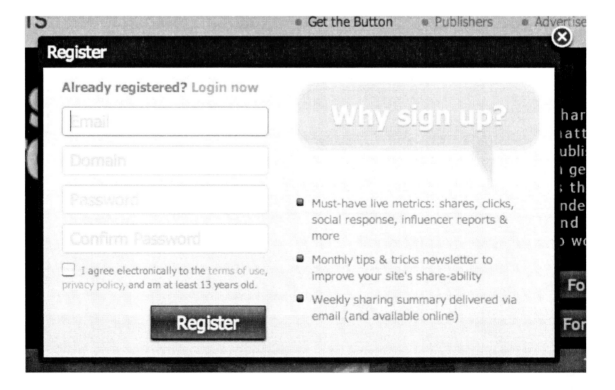

Part 5
Mobile: The future of Technology and Ministry

Let's Talk Strategy

The Mobile iChurch: The future is mobile. A great iChurch will go where everyone is.... No longer are internet users limited to computers plugged into their internet connection at home or work. Folks are now mobile, on the move, all day long. This year, more smartphones, tablets and mobile devices are being released than any other prior year. Soon, there will be more mobile users than desktop/laptop computer users. To reach all these users, your ministry must appear on mobile phones. When someone searches for God or Hope or Help from any device, your church needs to be there to answer them. With the mobile iChurch, you can do it.

I want to take a moment and tell you a true story about the power of mobile and the iChurch. Each day, cell phones are getting cheaper to make and competition grows fiercer. Cell phone manufacturers must move all these phones they keeping making. One day, some cell phone executive comes up with an idea to give phones away for free with the requirement that the user watch advertisements that appear on the cell phone screen. While the user of this free cell phone is talking, an advertisement shows up every sixty seconds. The user must hit a button to clear the ad and keep talking. The cell phone companies start giving them away in India. Many poor people who have no possessions or money take these phones. They must watch these advertisements for products they have no hope of ever buying. So who would be dumb enough to pay the phone company to advertise to a bunch of poor, homeless and hopeless people in India? Christian ministries, that's who! What do the Christian ministries' advertisements say to these poor people? "There is hope. Click here for hope." Once they click on the link, they are taken to a site that introduces them to Jesus. When they desire to engage in more conversation via phone or internet, someone who speaks their language is connected to answer their questions and minister to them. That's right. Poor people in India learn about Jesus through free mobile technology. Amazing!

Now imagine that "someone" who lives in your city, types into their smartphone "Is God real?" They see your iChurch on the search rankings and click on your website. Perhaps they send a text or email. Your staff instantly receives this inquiry at 8:30 p.m. and responds with an uplifting message directing them to a church service for more help. It happens every day.

How do get you there? First, you need a strategy. There needs to be a vision for the mobile presence of a ministry and how it will further the ministry. Let's look at the options your mobile iChurch has available.

A Mobile Site

When a smartphone user searches the internet and lands on a website that is not mobile optimized, the user sees the actual computer/laptop style website. The Wall Street Journal is a good example. When you explore that site, it isn't mobile optimized. You have to blow up individual sections just so you can read it. The Wall Street Journal has made a conscious decision not to have a mobile website. Most businesses, however, have made a decision to have a mobile website.

The advantages of a mobile website are self evident. When a smartphone user accesses a website that has a mobile site, everything fits. You can easily read the information and access the proper links without having to make size adjustments.

> **Geek tip:** Websites can be programmed to automatically show a different version (mobile or regular) of the website based on what type of device you are using. Whether it is a laptop, desktop, mobile device or tablet, a program called a "sniffer" detects the user's web viewing device and directs the mobile user to the mobile site instead of the normal full size website.

A good mobile website should include (but does not have to be limited to) the following pages:

- Home – This page should consist of links to the banners of current series and events.
- Locations and Service Times.
- Online Media.
    - Live services.
    - Archived Sermons or past TV shows.
    - Podcasts.
- Online Resources.
- Links to other ministry resources such as blogs or documents.
- Online bible.
- About Us.
    - About the Pastor.
    - About the church/ministry.
    - Volunteering/working at the ministry.
    - Mission/Vision statement.
- Online Giving.

Mobile Store

We explained the need for an online store in the eCommerce Part and now we simply add it to the mobile website. The idea here is to not only replicate your existing full-size website but connect to the buyer the moment he or she has an impulse to purchase. Your iChurch may have products such as books, podcasts or tickets to events that need to be sold. A mobile store will move more of these products. The key to a good mobile store is one that makes it easy for buyers to purchase your church's products and services. As stated in Part 3, the easiest way to create a mobile online store is to purchase an online store that has a mobile component/add-on. The store should automatically convert to mobile format when a user is viewing the online store from a mobile device.

Mobile Giving

Along the same lines as the mobile store, having the ability to accept donations from a mobile device greatly adds to your bottomline. As we stated in the eCommerce section, potential donors may be attending an event where your church is represented and decide to donate. Instead of waiting until they drive home, log on to the computer, access your website and then donate, bingo!....they have donated in seconds. Adding mobile giving to your iChurch is really a necessity. Mobile giving can be added to your mobile website using the ecommerce online donation solutions that were discussed in Part 3. These options include PayPal (paypal.com) and Kimbia (kimbia.com). Both of these can be optimized for mobile giving via your mobile website.

More Mobile Options

Once you have the basics such as a mobile website, mobile store and mobile giving, you may want to consider some optional applications.

Check-In - There are applications that use the GPS feature in a smartphone and allow a mobile user to check into a location. This essentially announces to the world that the smartphone user is at a particular location. Why would someone do this? With the explosion of social media, people want their friends to know what they are doing and where they are every minute of the day. The iChurch can take advantage of this "informational need" by allowing people to check-in and announce that they are now at your church or a church event. This brings exposure of your church to potential visitors. Examples of this are Facebook Places feature via mobile devices and Foursquare's mobile application.

Location-Based Coupons - Also using the GPS feature, this application can send the smartphone an instant coupon when he or she is near your facility or event or has checked-in, as stated above. Restaurants use location-based coupons to tempt customers as they drive by their location. The iChurch can use this service to send coupons for a discount to an event or the purchase of products. Location-Based coupons are a great way to increase sales of items that need to be moved or events that need to be filled up.

Examples of this are Facebook Places feature via mobile devices and Foursquare's mobile application.

Mobile Barcodes - Mobile barcodes are an interesting way to drive customer engagement and in-store transactions. Here's how they work. When retailers enable the mobile barcode functionality, customers can use the camera in their mobile phone to "scan" a picture of a barcode, which can then bring up a special landing page for that product or group of products. This can provide customers with instant product and pricing details and create opportunities for cross- or upselling. These same capabilities could also provide the ability to generate coupons that encourage impulse buying in the store. For churches large enough to have book stores or other retail space, this may be a good option by providing more information to the potential buyer and driving more sales.

Mobile Apps

As I touched on this a bit earlier, once you have a mobile website, you should then look at creating mobile applications for specific mobile devices. Mobile applications can create a much more engaging experience for mobile users because the application is native on their phone and not dependent on the internet or a mobile web browser. This approach has its advantages and disadvantages. The mobile ministry apps that I have on my iPhone are the Saddleback Church app, Elevation app, Cottonwood app, Mars Hill app, iHop-KC app and Harvest Church app. I won't get into specifics on how to create a mobile church app since I focus more on mobile websites in this book but here are three great companies that help ministries create awesome church mobile apps for iPhones, iPads and android devices.

- Phonegap.com
- Ro4r.com/churches/
- Thechurchapp.org

Multichannel Engagement

I want to conclude this Part by explaining the point made by this important sounding phrase, "Multichannel Engagement." What does this actually mean? There are multiple ways (or channels) to deal with customers. The customer can come into your store and browse. Or you can have a salesman in the store talk with them. The customer can call your company and talk on the phone. Or instant message with your sales staff. With most of these contact channels, the mobile device becomes the first point of contact with a potential customer. Once contact is established, the customer can then be transferred to a different online or offline channel. For example, a person uses their smartphone to send your staff a message about needing help in a marriage. The staff now sends them a notice or coupon for an upcoming seminar on marriages. The person is also directed to a community group and given the church times. Perhaps they are connected up to the family minister of the church who talks to them on the phone or mobile Skype. The mobile device has now opened up the engagement to multiple channels. This is the power of mobile and the future.

What I Want For My iChurch - Part 5

(a) I want an iChurch mobile website to have:

1. Home page with links to banners of the current series and events.

2. Locations and Service times.

3. Online Media with:

   o Live services.

   o Archived Sermons or past TV shows.

   o Podcasts.

4. Online Resources.

5. Links to other ministry resources such as blogs or documents.

6. Online bible.

7. About Us with:

   o About the Pastor.
   o About the church/ministry.
   o Volunteering/working at the ministry.
   o Mission/Vision statement.

8. Mobile Giving.

9. Mobile Store.

10. Check in feature.

11. Location-based coupons.

12. Mobile barcodes.

13. Mobile Apps.

Let's Talk Tech

When you design a mobile website, you must make sure it works on all the smartphones by testing it. A good strategy is to create a mobile site based on webkit 2 (or 3) standards using HTML5, CSS and JavaScript (JQuery). This will ensure that your mobile website will be viewable on all new smartphones. The newest smartphones (iPhone, Android, and Windows) come equipped with webkit enabled browsers that have functionality very similar to computers and laptops. Once the mobile website is complete, you can then convert the mobile site to mobile apps for iOS, android, windows and blackberry (we will get to this in the tech talk section). Chart 5a below shows the breakdown of the smartphone market according to percentages. Apple iOS and Google Android OS are tied at 40% each, Blackberry RIM OS is next with 14% and the rest make up the final 6% of the market.

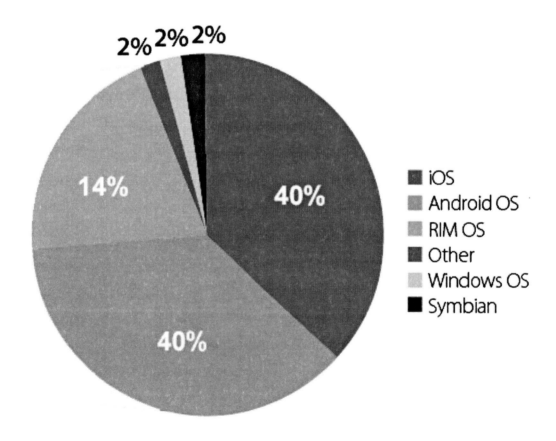

When it comes to mobile ministry websites, there are two that I use the most. The first is Lifechurch Mobile (http://m.lifechurch.tv) which was built using Jquery mobile. The second website is TD Jakes Mobile (http://www.tdjakes.org/mobile) which was built using HTML and CSS.

There are numerous ways you can create a mobile website. You can program it from scratch making sure you code your website to match each device to both width and heigth. Also, you can use a mobile website template and fill in your ministry's information based on the layout of the template. Another way is to create a Content Management System that has a mobile layout. With this, you create a normal website using the Content Management System. When an online user comes to your website from a mobile device, the CMS automatically recognizes the mobile device and displays the website using the mobile layout instead of the normal layout.

Of the numerous ways to create a mobile website, I have found that there are two that are relatively easy. The first way is to use a Content Management System such as wordpress to create a website and add an addon/widget called Wptouch that automatically displays the website in a mobile format when a user comes to your website on a mobile device. The second way is to use a mobile template package such as iWebkit (http://snippetspace.com/projects/iwebkit/) and build your mobile website based on that. We will explain both approaches in this tech talk section.

Wordpress Mobile Plugin

In Part 1 - Let's Talk Tech section, I explained how to install a WordPress CMS using Godaddy Hosting. To setup your mobile website using Wordpress, you first need to login and get to your Dashboard page. In the left column click on the **Plugins** tab. When it expands, click on the **Add New** link.

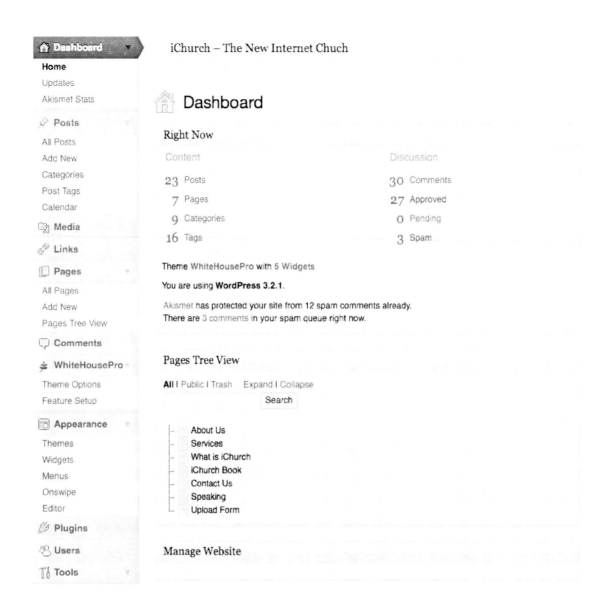

iChurch – The New Internet Chuch

This will take you to the **Install Plugins** page where you can search for the **Wptouch** plugin. Type **Wptouch** into the search box and click on the **Search Plugins** button.

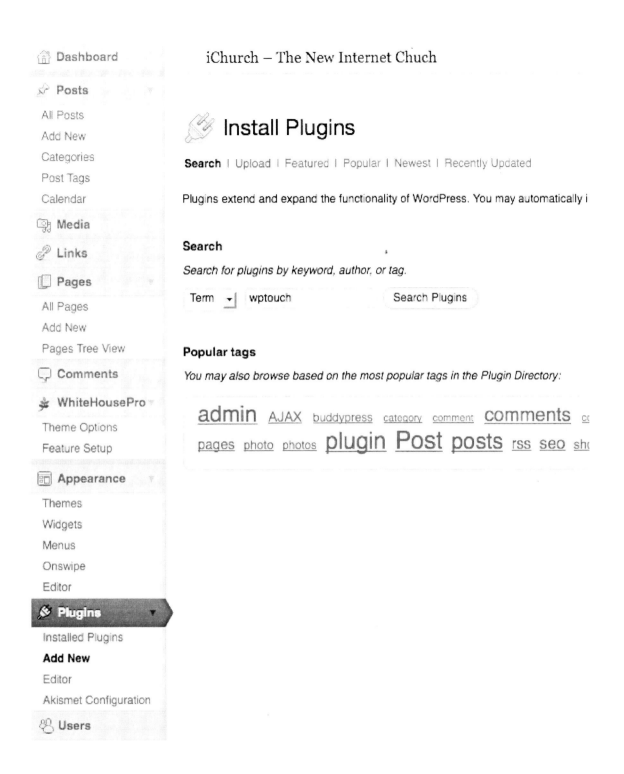

Once you get to this page you will see WPtouch as the top option. Click the **Install Now** link and Wordpress will automatically install the WPtouch plugin. This will make your website mobile compatible. The final step is to go to the left column again, click the **Installed Plugins** and scroll down to **WPtouch** to make sure it's activated. If you see the

Activate link then click it. If you see a **Deactivate link** then its already activated and you are good to go.

Create Your Own Mobile Website using iWebkit

If you don't have a CMS like Wordpress, you can create your own mobile website. There are numerous ways to create a mobile website but I will focus on one that I found was quite easy to use: iWebkit (http://snippetspace.com/projects/iwebkit/). WebKit is accessible to anyone, even those with little html knowledge. It is simple to understand thanks to the included user guide. In a couple of minutes you will have created a profesional looking website. iWebKit is the framework of choice because besides being easy to use, it loads extremely fast, is compatible with numerous mobile devices and is extendable. It is simple html that anyone can handle. Simplicity is the key!

When you click on the **Download button** you get a zip file that's named "iWebKit5.04.zip" (this was the file name while I was writing this book, new versions may be released and named accordingly). Once the zip file is downloaded, double-click on it to open the file and "extract" the files to your desktop. Here are the files that you will see inside.

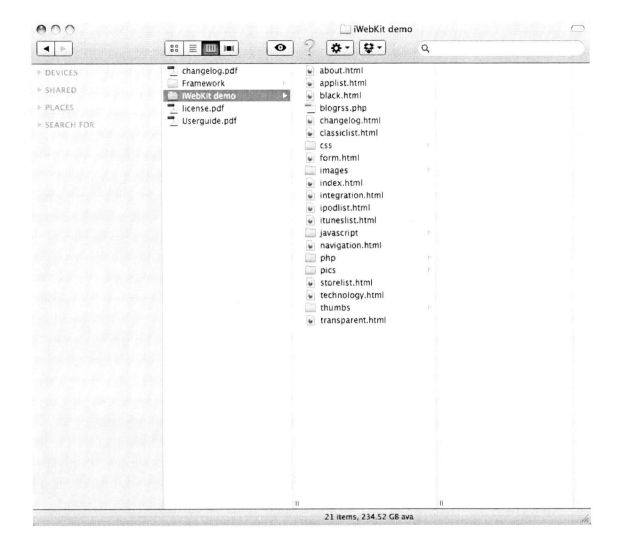

Based on these files, I want to point out a few things that will make this process much easier for you. 1. You have a user guide that comes with this download. It's **Userguide.pdf** and it walks you through the process of creating a mobile website using this software. 2. The **Framework** folder has a blank template that you can go in and customize however you like. It's basically a start from scratch template. 3. The **iWebkit demo** folder is the actual demo from the iWebkit website. The files in this folder are already programmed to look like what you see in the online demo and you can go in to alter and recode them to meet the mobile website needs of your ministry. When I used iWebkit to create a website for a ministry, I actually read the **Userguide.pdf** manual and then went into the **iWebkit demo** folder and recoded the files from the demo website. That was the easiest approach. Now let's look at some of the files that I recoded so that you can see how I did it.

First File:index.html - the index file was the first file that I focused on. Here is the index file for the demo website. From top to bottom, notice how it has 3 buttons at the top, a Features subheader and another header in blue with some text about the following options that you can click. The options have an icon in front of them and an arrow to the right that shows you can click them. Even further down the page are larger icons with arrows to the right that show you can click those as well.

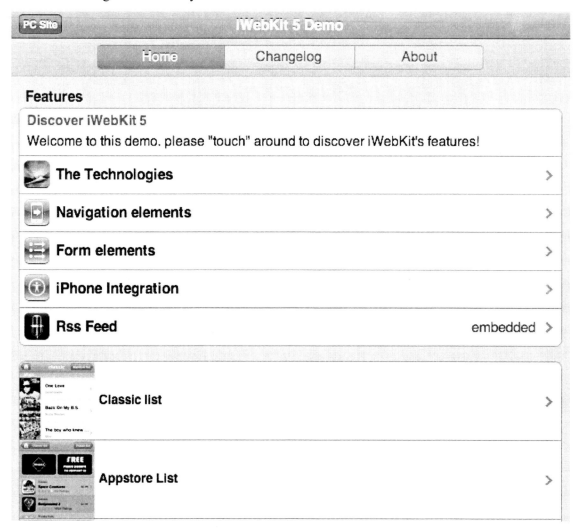

Here is the index.html page that I created for the mobile website for Crenshaw Christian Center. You can see that I changed a few things from the demo version. I will explain more detail below the picture.

First, I changed the top bar from a solid blue to a transparent black. To do this I changed the code in the original index file:

```
<div id="topbar">
```

and updated it to

```
<div id="topbar" class="transparent">
```

Next I removed the title "iWebkit 5 Demo" from the top bar by changing this code:

```
<div id="title"> iWebKit 5 Demo</div>
```

and updated it to

```
<div id="title">  </div>
```

Right underneath that line of code I added a button that was to appear on the right side of the top transparent bar. That would be the donation button. I inserted this line of code to complete that.

```
<div id="rightbutton"><a href="donate.html" class="noeffect">Donate</a> </div>
```

Next, I wanted to remove the three buttons "Home, Changelog and About" from the top and replace them with the EIFM logo. I completed that by removing this code:

```
<div id="tributton">
<div class="links">
<a id="pressed" href="#">Home</a><a href="changelog.html">Changelog</a><a
href="about.html">About</a>
</div> </div>
```

and inserted this code

```
<div class="links">
<div style="text-align:center">
<img src="images/eiflogo.png" />
</div> </div>
```

Then, I wanted to remove the standard verbiage of "Features" and "Discover iWebkit 5, Welcome to this demo, please 'touch' around to discover iWebkit's features!" This was replaced with "Ever Increasing Faith Mobile" and Apostle Price's online website greeting. To do this I changed the code below.

```
<div id="content">
<span class="graytitle">Features</span>
<ul class="pageitem">
<li class="textbox"><span class="header">Discover iWebKit 5</span>
<p> Welcome to this demo. please &quot;touch&quot; around to discover iWebKit's
features!</p> </li>
```

and inserted this code

```
<div id="content">
<span class="graytitle">Ever Increasing Faith Mobile</span>
<ul class="pageitem">
<li class="textbox">
<p>Greetings in the matchless name of Jesus Christ. Thank you for joining Ever Increasing Faith
Ministries on the Mobile Web. It is exciting to be able to minister to you through this vast
information network. My hope is that our Mobile Website will be a valuable tool in bringing you
ever closer to the Lord Jesus Christ.</p> </li>
```

Next, we needed to update the icons and links that are on the demo index.html page to match icons and links that we would use for this website. I changed "The Technologies" to "Live Service" and "Navigation elements" to "Online Media." Here is the code I used.

```
<li class="menu"><a href="technology.html"> <img src="thumbs/plugin.png" />
<span class="name">The  Technologies</span><span class="arrow"></span></a></li>

<li class="menu"><a href="navigation.html"><img src="thumbs/start.png" />
<span class="name">Navigation elements</span><span class="arrow"></span></a></li>

<li class="menu"><a href="form.html"> <img src="thumbs/other.png" />
<span class="name">Form elements</span><span class="arrow"></span></a></li>
```

and inserted this code

```
<li class="menu"><a href="live.html"><img src="thumbs/voice.png" />
<span class="name">Live Service</span><span class="arrow"></span></a></li>

<li class="menu"><a href="media.html"><img src="thumbs/video.png" />
<span class="name">Online Media</span><span class="arrow"></span></a></li>

<li class="menu"><a href="donate.html"><img src="thumbs/stocks.png" />
<span class="name">Donate</span><span class="arrow"></span></a></li>
```

Next I deleted all the code from the bottom list with the large icons. I didn't need that code at the time but I would save that code for when I created my broadcasts.html page that we will look at later. Anyhow, I deleted all this code from the demo index.html

```
<ul class="pageitem">
<li class="store"><a href="classiclist.html"><span class="image" style="background-image:
url('pics/classiclist.png')"></span> <span class="name">Classic list</span><span
class="arrow"></span></a></li>
<li class="store"><a href="applist.html"><span class="image" style="background-image:
url('pics/applist.png')"></span> <span class="name">Appstore List</span><span
class="arrow"></span></a></li>
<li class="store"><a href="storelist.html"><span class="image" style="background-image:
url('pics/ituneslist.png')"></span> <span class="name">iTunes classic list</span><span
class="arrow"></span></a></li>
<li class="store"><a href="ituneslist.html"><span class="image" style="background-image:
url('pics/itunesmusiclist.png')"></span> <span class="name">iTunes music list</span><span
class="arrow"></span></a></li>
<li class="store"><a href="ipodlist.html"><span class="image" style="background-image:
url('pics/ipodlist.png')"></span> <span class="name">iPod List</span><span
class="arrow"></span></a></li>
</ul>
```

Finally, I changed the footer on the demo page and added the footer information from the faithdome.org website which was the EIF copyright information. Here is the code I changed.

```
<div id="footer"> <a href="http://iwebkit.net">Powered by iWebKit</a></div></body></html>
```

and inserted this code.

```
<div id="footer">&copy; Ever Increasing Faith Ministries | <a class="noeffect"
href="contactus.html">Contact Us</a> </div>
```

Second File:broadcasts.html – To create the broadcasts.html file for the CCC mobile website, I took the storelist.html file in the iWebkit5.04 folder and customized it into a

174

broadcast.html file that you can click to watch broadcasts of the EIF TV show from your mobile device. Take a look at the storelist.html file below

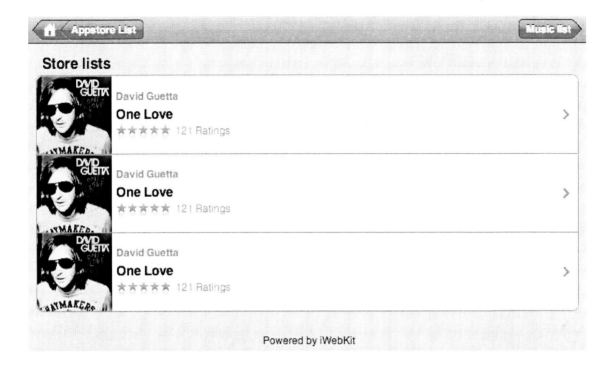

Now let's look at the broadcasts.html file that was created from this file.

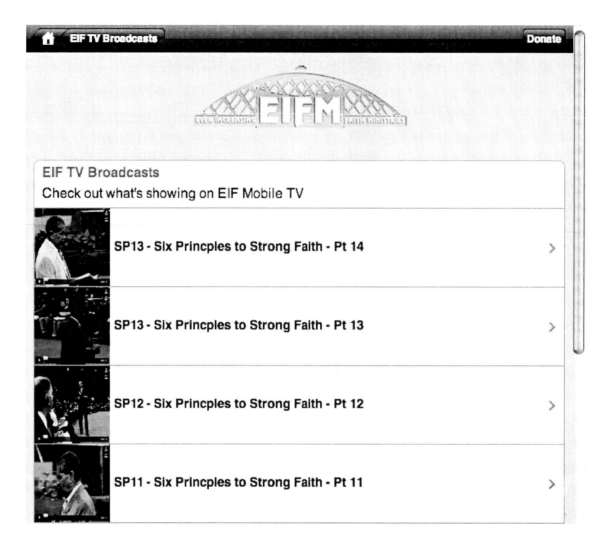

First, just like the index.html page, we changed the top bar to transparent, added a donate button to the right and insert the EIFM logo. But notice that in the top bar where it originally said "Appstore List", we changed that to say "EIF TV Broadcasts." Here is the code we changed in the storelist.html file to complete that.

```
<div id="topbar">
<div id="leftnav"> <a href="index.html"><img alt="home" src="images/home.png" /></a>
<a href="applist.html">Appstore  List</a></div>
<div id="rightnav"> <a href="ituneslist.html">Music list</a></div> </div>
```

and updated it to

```
<div id="topbar" class="transparent">
<div id="leftnav"><a href="index.html"><img alt="home" src="images/home.png" /></a>
<a href="broadcasts.html">EIF TV Broadcasts</a></div>
<div id="rightbutton"><a href="donate.html" class="noeffect">Donate</a> </div> </div>
```

Next, I removed the "Store Lists" Header and inserted the "EIF TV Broadcasts" subheader as well as the "Check out what's showing on EIF Mobile TV" verbiage. Here is the code I used to complete that.

```
<div id="content">
<span class="graytitle">Store lists</span> <ul class="pageitem">
<li class="store"><a class="noeffect" href="http://itunes.apple.com/us/album/blood-sugar-sex-magik-bonus-track/id309577455"> <span class="image" style="background-image:
url('http://a1.phobos.apple.com/us/r1000/002/Music/0e/f0/26/mzi.bxbwyvvz.170x170-75.jpg')"></span><span class="comment">Red Hot Chili Peppers</span><span
class="name">Blood    Sugar Sex Magik</span><span class="stars5"></span><span
class="starcomment">151  Ratings</span><span class="arrow"></span></a></li>


<li class="store"><a class="noeffect" href="http://itunes.apple.com/fr/album/back-on-my-b-s/id314164974"><span class="image" style="background-image:
url('http://a1.phobos.apple.com/us/r2000/005/Music/c6/3e/f8/mzi.kfqhjocj.170x170-75.jpg')"></span><span class="comment">Busta Rhymes</span><span class="name">Back  On
My B.S.</span><span class="stars4"></span><span class="starcomment">404
Ratings</span><span class="arrow"></span></a></li>
```

and updated it to

```
<div id="content">
<ul class="pageitem">
<li class="textbox"><span class="header">EIF TV Broadcasts</span><p>Check out what's
showing on EIF Mobile TV</p></li>
<li class="store"><a href="sp14.html"><span class="image" style="background-image:
url('images/sp14.jpg')"></span><span class="name">SP14 - Six Princples to Strong Faith - Pt
14</span><span class="arrow"></span></a></li>
```

<li class="store"><a href="sp13.html"><span class="image" style="background-image: url('images/sp13.jpg')"></span><span class="name">SP13 - Six Princples to Strong Faith - Pt 13</span><span class="arrow"></span></a></li>

Once I added all of the images and put in links to the video pages, I then updated the footer in the index.html file and this page was complete.

Third file: about.html - Now let's look at the about.html file in the iWebkit5.04 folder. This file is the basis for the video pages and the donation page for CCC mobile website. This about.html page included the three buttons at the top and just a single box of content beneath it.

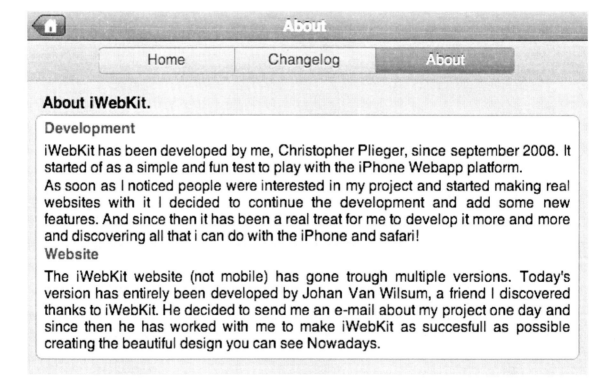

Now let's look at one of the video pages, sp14.html, that I created from this about.html page.

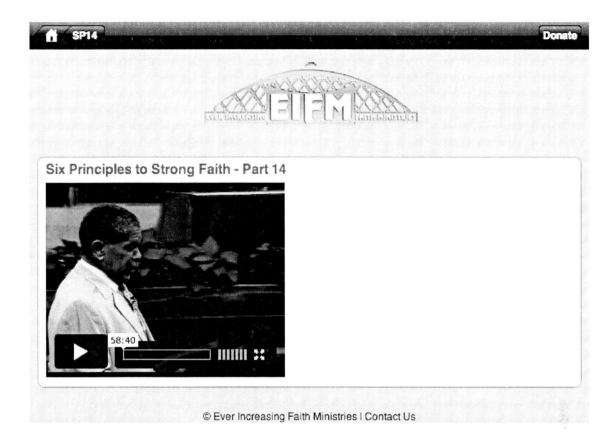

In order to create one of the video pages sp14.html, first, just like the index.html page, I changed the top bar to transparent, added a donate button to the right, inserted the EIFM logo and removed the header as you have seen in other pages above. To set this page up, I changed the subheader from "Development" to "Six Principles to Strong Faith – Part 14" and inserted a vimeo video beneath it. Here is the code I changed in the about.html file to complete that.

<div id="content"> <span class="graytitle">About iWebKit.</span>

<ul class="pageitem"> <li class="textbox">

<span class="header">Development</span>

<p>iWebKit has been developed by me, Christopher Plieger, since september 2008. It started of as a simple and fun test to play with the iPhone Webapp platform.</p>

<p>As soon as I noticed people were interested in my project and started making real websites with it I decided to continue the development and add some new features. And since then it has been a real treat for me to develop it more and more and discovering all that i can do with the iPhone and safari!</p>

\<span class="header"\>Website\</span\>\<p\>The iWebKit website (not mobile) has gone trough multiple versions. Today's version has entirely been developed by Johan Van Wilsum, a friend I discovered thanks to iWebKit. He decided to send me an e-mail about my project one day and since then he has worked with me to make iWebKit as succesfull as possible creating the beautiful design you can see Nowadays.\</p\>

\</li\> \</ul\> \</div\>

and updated it to

\<div id="content"\>

\<ul class="pageitem"\> \<li class="textbox"\>

\<span class="header"\>Six Principles to Strong Faith - Part 14\</span\>

\<p\> \<iframe src="http://player.vimeo.com/video/28345292?byline=0&portrait=0" width="285" height="225" frameborder="0"\>\</iframe\> \</p\>

\</li\>\</ul\>\</div\>

Take notice that the video file code

\<iframe src="http://player.vimeo.com/video/28345292?byline=0&portrait=0" width="285" height="225" frameborder="0"\>\</iframe\>

is what we obtained from vimeo.com. We used vimeo for our mobile website because it is HTML5 compatible. Likewise, you can use YouTube.com \<iframe\> code that you get from their website since they are HTML5 compatible. The reason I use vimeo is because YouTube has a 20 minute time limit for videos and the weekly sermons are about 58 minutes. Thus, I needed a provider without a time limit and I chose vimeo.com. Once I added the video file, I then updated the footer like in the index.html file and this page was complete.

Now let's look at the donate.html page which was also created from the about.html code.

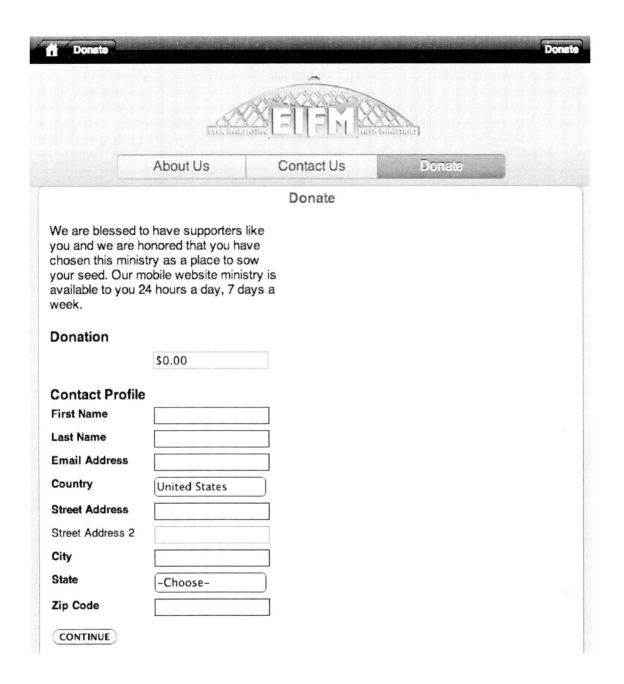

In order to create the donate.html, first, just like the index.html page, I changed the top bar to transparent, added a donate button to the right, inserted the EIFM logo and removed the header as you have seen in other pages above. To set this page up I changed the subheader from "Development" to "Donate" and centered it. I then added a donation module from Kimbia.com which is what CCC uses instead of Paypal.com. Here is the code I changed in the about.html file to complete that.

<div id="content"> <span class="graytitle">About iWebKit.</span>

<ul class="pageitem"> <li class="textbox">

<span class="header">Development</span>

<p>iWebKit has been developed by me, Christopher Plieger, since september 2008. It started of as a simple and fun test to play with the iPhone Webapp platform.</p>

<p>As soon as I noticed people were interested in my project and started making real websites with it I decided to continue the development and add some new features. And since then it has been a real treat for me to develop it more and more and discovering all that i can do with the iPhone and safari!</p>

<span class="header">Website</span><p>The iWebKit website (not mobile) has gone trough multiple versions. Today&#39;s version has entirely been developed by Johan Van Wilsum, a friend I discovered thanks to iWebKit. He decided to send me an e-mail about my project one day and since then he has worked with me to make iWebKit as succesfull as possible creating the beautiful design you can see Nowadays.</p>

</li> </ul> </div>

and updated it to

<div id="content">

<ul class="pageitem"> <li class="textbox">

<span class="header">Donate</span>

<p><script
src='https://widgets.kimbia.com/widgets/form.js?channel=crenshawchristiancenter/mobile'></script></p>

</li></ul> </div>

Take notice that the donation code

<script
src='https://widgets.kimbia.com/widgets/form.js?channel=crenshawchristiancenter/mobile'></script>

is what I obtained from kimbia.com. I used kimbia.com for our mobile website because it is HTML5 compatible. Likewise, you can use PayPal.com donation code that you get from their website since they are HTML5 compatible. Once I added the donate code, I updated the footer like in the index.html file and this page was complete.

Fourth File: integration.html – Finally, take a look at this file when you are looking through the files in the iWebkit5.04 folder. The integration file has great options of how to interact with the phone within the code. Look at the page below and the code beneath it. It will help you if you want to create a mobile website that interacts with the users' mobile device more in depth.

```
<div id="content">
<span class="graytitle">Integration</span>
<ul class="pageitem">
<li class="menu"> <a class="noeffect"
href="mailto:test@test.com?cc=ex@ample.net,lisa@wwdc.com&amp;subject=Greetings from
www.iwebkit.mobi!&amp;body=See how cool this is!"> <img alt="mail" src="thumbs/mail.png"
/><span class="name">Mail</span><span class="arrow"></span></a></li>


<li class="menu"> <a class="noeffect"
href="http://phobos.apple.com/WebObjects/MZStore.woa/wa/viewAlbum?id=287810321&amp;s
=143442"> <img alt="itunes" src="thumbs/itunes.png" /><span
class="name">iTunes</span><span class="arrow"></span></a></li>
```

```html
<li class="menu"> <a class="noeffect" href="http://www.itunes.com/app/CameraBag"> <img alt="appstore" src="thumbs/appstore.png" /><span class="name">Appstore</span><span class="arrow"></span></a></li>

<li class="menu"><a class="noeffect" href="sms:12125551212"><img alt="sms" src="thumbs/messages.png" /><span class="name">SMS</span><span class="comment">iPhone  Only</span><span class="arrow"></span></a></li>

<li class="menu"><a class="noeffect" href="tel:408-555-5555"> <img alt="telephone" src="thumbs/telephone.png" /><span class="name">Telephone/Contact</span><span class="arrow"></span></a></li>

<li class="menu"> <a class="noeffect" href="http://www.youtube.com/watch?v=DWmQEv0oF08"> <img alt="YouTube" src="thumbs/youtube.png" /><span class="name">YouTube</span><span class="arrow"></span></a></li>

<li class="menu"><a class="noeffect" href="http://maps.google.com/maps/ms?f=q&amp;hl=fr&amp;geocode=&amp;ie=UTF8&amp;msa=0&amp;msid=10643132918913945243l.000458c25e140ead6df80&amp;ll=43.313438,3.417091&amp;spn=0.084934,0.22316&amp;z=13"><img alt="google maps" src="thumbs/maps.png" /><span class="name">Google Maps</span><span class="arrow"></span></a></li>
</ul> </div>
```

Mobile Browser Detection

Once you have completed your mobile website you can start telling your online users to go to the mobile website by giving them your mobile web address which could be www.yourchurch.com/mobile. But there is an easier way to get people to automatically go to your mobile website when they come to your current website on their mobile device. This process is called "browser detection" and "browser redirection." Basically, when an online user comes to your website from any device, laptop, desktop, mobile phone or tablet, the website can detect what type of device it is via the web browser. If you use a program called a "browser sniffer," you can detect mobile devices automatically and direct them to your newly created mobile website.

Here's how you do it. Go to DetectMobileBrowser.com (http://detectmobilebrowser.com/). Here there are a variety of coding choices you can use to automatically detect mobile devices and redirect them. If your regular website (or server) is created in PHP, you can use the PHP code snippet to redirect people. Likewise, if your regular website (or server) is created in ASP.NET, you can use the ASP.NET (or C#) code snippet to redirect people.

Detect Mobile Browsers | Open source mobile phone detection

No mobile browser detected.

Mozilla/5.0 (Macintosh; Intel Mac OS X 10_6_8) AppleWebKit/535.1 (KHTML, like Gecko) Chrome/13.0.782.215 Safari/535.1

Download Scripts

Apache | ASP | ASP.NET | ColdFusion | C# | IIS | JSP | JavaScript | jQuery | nginx | node.js | PHP | Perl | Python | Rails

Redirect Mobile Browsers

If it's *not* a mobile browser, take them to:

Otherwise, send them to:

Let's click the PHP button and download the PHP code for a redirect. You will get a download file called **detectmobilebrowser.php.txt**. When you open this file, you will see the following code:

```php
<?php
$useragent=$_SERVER['HTTP_USER_AGENT'];

if(preg_match('/android.+mobile|avantgo|bada\/|blackberry|blazer|compal|elaine|fennec|hiptop|ie
mobile|ip(hone|od)|iris|kindle|lge |maemo|midp|mmp|opera m(ob|in)i|palm(
os)?|phone|p(ixi|re)\/|plucker|pocket|psp|symbian|treo|up\.(browser|link)|vodafone|wap|windows
(ce|phone)|xda|xiino/i',$useragent)||preg_match('/1207|6310|6590|3gso|4thp|50[1-6]i|770s|802s|a
wa|abac|ac(er|oo|s\-)|ai(ko|rn)|al(av|ca|co)|amoi|an(ex|ny|yw)|aptu|ar(ch|go)|as(te|us)|attw|au(di|\-
m|r |s )|avan|be(ck|ll|nq)|bi(lb|rd)|bl(ac|az)|br(e|v)w|bumb|bw\-(n|u)|c55\/|capi|ccwa|cdm\-
|cell|chtm|cldc|cmd\-|co(mp|nd)|craw|da(it|ll|ng)|dbte|dc\-s|devi|dica|dmob|do(c|p)o|ds(12|\-
d)|el(49|ai)|em(l2|ul)|er(ic|k0)|esl8|ez([4-7]0|os|wa|ze)|fetc|fly(\-|_)|g1 u|g560|gene|gf\-5|g\-
mo|go(\.w|od)|gr(ad|un)|haie|hcit|hd\-(m|p|t)|hei\-|hi(pt|ta)|hp( i|ip)|hs\-c|ht(c(\-|
|_|a|g|p|s|t)|tp)|hu(aw|tc)|i\-(20|go|ma)|i230|iac( |\-
|\/)|ibro|idea|ig01|ikom|im1k|inno|ipaq|iris|ja(t|v)a|jbro|jemu|jigs|kddi|keji|kgt( |\/)|klon|kpt |kwc\-
|kyo(c|k)|le(no|xi)|lg( g|\/(k|l|u)|50|54|e\-|e\/|\-[a-w])|libw|lynx|m1\-
w|m3ga|m50\/|ma(te|ui|xo)|mc(01|21|ca)|m\-cr|me(di|rc|ri)|mi(o8|oa|ts)|mmef|mo(01|02|bi|de|do|t(\-
| |o|v)|zz)|mt(50|p1|v )|mwbp|mywa|n10[0-2]|n20[2-3]|n30(0|2)|n50(0|2|5)|n7(0(0|1)|10)|ne((c|m)\-
|on|tf|wf|wg|wt)|nok(6|i)|nzph|o2im|op(ti|wv)|oran|owg1|p800|pan(a|d|t)|pdxg|pg(13|\-([1-
8]|c))|phil|pire|pl(ay|uc)|pn\-2|po(ck|rt|se)|prox|psio|pt\-g|qa\-a|qc(07|12|21|32|60|\-[2-7]|i\-
)|qtek|r380|r600|raks|rim9|ro(ve|zo)|s55\/|sa(ge|ma|mm|ms|ny|va)|sc(01|h\-|oo|p\-)|sdk\/|se(c(\-
|0|1)|47|mc|nd|ri)|sgh\-|shar|sie(\-|m)|sk\-0|sl(45|id)|sm(al|ar|b3|it|t5)|so(ft|ny)|sp(01|h\-|v\-|v
)|sy(01|mb)|t2(18|50)|t6(00|10|18)|ta(gt|lk)|tcl\-|tdg\-|tel(i|m)|tim\-|t\-mo|to(pl|sh)|ts(70|m\-
|m3|m5)|tx\-9|up(\.b|g1|si)|utst|v400|v750|veri|vi(rg|te)|vk(40|5[0-3]|\-
v)|vm40|voda|vulc|vx(52|53|60|61|70|80|81|83|85|98)|w3c(\-| )|webc|whit|wi(g
|nc|nw)|wmlb|wonu|x700|xda(\-|2|g)|yas\-|your|zeto|zte\-/i',substr($useragent,0,4)))

header('Location: http://detectmobilebrowser.com/mobile');
?>
```

186